A LONG WALK WITH THE MINOR PROPHETS

24 In-Depth Bible Studies on the Twelve Minor Prophets (Including a Featured Song about Each Prophet)

Jay McCluskey

All Scripture quotations, unless otherwise indicated, are taken from the Holy Bible, New International Version®, NIV®. Copyright ©1973, 1978, 1984, 2011 by Biblica, Inc.™ Used by permission of Zondervan. All rights reserved worldwide. www.zondervan.comThe "NIV" and "New International Version" are trademarks registered in the United States Patent and Trademark Office by Biblica, Inc.™

Copyright © 2024 Jay McCluskey
All rights reserved.
ISBN: 9798324539436

TABLE OF CONTENTS

ACKNOWLEDGEMENTS v
INTRODUCTION vii
1. OBADIAH 17
2. JOEL 29
3. JONAH 1-2 41
4. JONAH 3-4 51
5. AMOS 1-2 63
6. AMOS 3-5 79
7. AMOS 7-9 91
8. HOSEA 1-3 101
9. HOSEA 4-6 111
10. HOSEA 7-10 121
11. HOSEA 11-14 133
12. MICAH 1-2 147
13. MICAH 3-5 161
14. MICAH 6-7 173
15. NAHUM 1-3 189
16. ZEPHANIAH 1-3 205
17. HABUKKUK 1-3 225
18. HAGGAI 1-2 239
19. ZECHARIAH 1-6 255
20. ZECHARIAH 7-8 271
21. ZECHARIAH 9-14 283
22. MALACHI 1-2 299
23. MALACHI 3-4 311

A Long Walk with the Minor Prophets

ACKNOWLEDGEMENTS

Approximately two decades ago, I adopted the practice of preparing and teaching extended Bible Studies (20-25 lessons) during my church's midweek gatherings. This pattern gave an approach that roughly follows the school year (September through May). At first, these long studies focused on entire books of the Bible such as Mark, John, Genesis, Acts, Revelation, and Isaiah. As the years went by, other long formats emerged such as The Parables of Jesus, The Life of David, and Women in the Bible. In time, I came to refer to these studies as "long walks" through different books and themes.

During my most recent quest to choose a "long walk" series for 2023-24, I opted to pursue my first "multi-book" study on The Minor Prophets. Frankly, I chose these writings to compel me to learn more about the ministry of these lesser-known representatives among God's messengers. I needed "brushing up" on the times and ministries of these twelve prophets.

The McCluskey family loves to travel! We especially enjoy sharing adventures along with other people. Mutual experiences alongside others enhances the joy of the journey! The same is true for an excursion through scripture. The presence, insights, and contributions of others are abundantly fulfilling. Let me note some of my fellow travelers.

Deep appreciation goes to the devoted members of our mid-week Bible Study classes. They are exceptionally faithful in their attendance. Some of them attend with me at 7:00 AM! These saints experience the first "rough drafts" of these lessons. And without fail, they offer useful insights, perspectives, and singing voices to the book you now hold.

A Long Walk with the Minor Prophets

To borrow the words in Malachi 3:17, they are "my treasured possession."

Thanks also to Violet Rice for her valuable proofreading contributions. For six months, our Sunday morning routine included this simple exchange: She returned a corrected chapter to me while I presented her with an unedited lesson for review. You will encounter her handiwork on virtually every page of this book.

I also salute Dr. Don Garner, retired Old Testament professor at Carson-Newman University. As I note in the Introduction, Dr. Garner's undergraduate class in Old Testament Prophets enhanced my respect and appreciation for this part of scripture. And I am so glad I kept those class notes!

Finally, my deep gratitude goes to you for reading this book. Whether you use these writings as a Bible study series or a resource for insights into individual prophets, I pray the Lord will grant you richer and deeper insights in your pursuit of truth. Come now as we take a long walk together through the Minor Prophets.

Jay McCluskey, DMin
Pastor, North Cleveland Baptist Church
Cleveland, TN

INTRODUCTION

When I was in elementary school, a dear Sunday School teacher was Doris Antrican. She challenged the kids in her class to memorize the books of the Bible in order. She offered a piece of hard candy for each book we could recite in order. With this incentive before me, I first learned all 27 books of the New Testament. On the Sunday we were to show our progress, my friend Rocky Hodge announced he could say the books of the New Testament forward AND BACKWARDS. After a quick mental review, I realized I could do that too. Mrs. Antrican agreed to give us a piece of candy for each New Testament book we named forward AND backward. That day, I left Sunday School with a bag of 54 pieces of candy. Weeks later, we repeated the feat, listing the books of the Old Testament backwards and forwards! That week's take home bag contained 78 pieces of candy. My mother jokingly threatened to send Mrs. Antrican my dentist bill after I ate all that sugar.

Today, when I recite the books of the Bible, I build on the foundation Doris Antrican helped establish. But I confess, my memory fails me when I get to the Minor Prophets.

Before pastors preach to our congregations, we first preach to ourselves. Before we share a truth from scripture, we receive it in our own hearts. With that in mind, I honestly approached the idea of studying the Minor Prophets because this is a part of the Bible about which I personally was a bit "rusty."

Upon learning the books of the Bible in order, a student of scripture quickly realizes that the writings of scripture are generally, but not exactly, in chronological order. The same is true for the Minor Prophets. Because it is useful to follow the flow of Hebrew history through the prophets' individual

A Long Walk with the Minor Prophets

ministries, our study will approach these writings in this Chronological Order.

THE PROPHETS IN CHRONOLOGICAL ORDER
(with Minor Prophets in bold-face type)

845 BC?	***Obadiah***
830 BC	***Joel***
780-750 BC	***Jonah***
760-750 BC	***Amos***
760-710 BC	***Hosea***
740-690 BC	Isaiah
735-700 BC	***Micah***
650-612 BC	***Nahum***
627-585 BC	Jeremiah
625 BC	***Zephaniah***
612-606 BC	***Habakkuk***
606-536 BC	Daniel
592-570 BC	Ezekiel
585 BC	Lamentations
520 BC	***Haggai***
520-518 BC	***Zechariah***
445-425 BC	***Malachi***

POINTS TO REMEMBER

The Old Testament Prophets refer to 17 Books covering the ministry of 16 Prophets.

The author of Lamentations, Jeremiah, is recognized as the only writer of two books. These 16 men all appear to be of Jewish descent. Regarding the Minor Prophets, we know very little about most of them.

The books of the Old Testament Prophets covered the time the Hebrew people were under the leadership of a King.

In a sense, the King was the political and military leader of the people. During this time, God raised up prophets to be spiritual leaders and royal counselors.

The 17 books of the Prophets cover a 400-year span from roughly 850 B.C. to 425 B.C.:

- Five books were written between the death of Solomon and the fall of the Northern Kingdom.
- Six books were written prior to the fall of the Southern Kingdom.
- Two books were written during the Babylonian Exile.
- Four books were written after the return from Babylonian captivity.

There WERE prophets in other times of Biblical history beyond the times of the Major and Minor Prophets.

Biblical references to *prophets* who did NOT live during the time of the Hebrew kings include:

- Moses (Deuteronomy 34:10)
- Aaron (Exodus 7:1)
- Miriam (Exodus 15:20)
- Deborah (Judges 4:4)
- John the Baptist (Matthew 14:5)
- The four daughters of Philip the Evangelist (Acts 21:9)

There WERE other prophets during the season of the Major and Minor Prophets, yet without a book of the Bible in his/her name.

These include servants such as: Nathan, Elijah, Elisha, and Huldah.

Prophets voiced powerful and strong directives from the Lord.

Some people have the personality of a priest. These people are mediators who facilitate peace between two parties. Biblical priests offered sacrifices between rebellious humans and a holy God. Other people receive the personality of a prophet. Biblical prophets spoke with boldness, power, and conviction. The prelude to their declarations was "Thus says the Lord." So great was their compulsion, they could not hold back their message. Jeremiah, who suffered greatly despite his faithful delivery of God's message, put it this way:

But if I say, "I will not mention his word or speak anymore in his name," his word is in my heart like a fire, a fire shut up in my bones. I am weary of holding it in; indeed, I cannot. Jeremiah 20:9 NIV.

IMPORTANT DATES

This table and chart give significant dates during the season of history we will follow. Note the years, the dominant empires on the world's stage, and the story of the Hebrew people during these times.

1020 BC	Establishment of Kingdom of Israel
950 BC	Division of Hebrews into Israel and Judah

A Long Walk with the Minor Prophets

722 BC	Fall of Israel to Assyria
612 BC	Fall of Assyria to Babylon
584 BC	Fall of Judah
539 BC	Fall of the Babylonian Empire to Persia
538 BC	Cyrus of Persia allows Hebrews to Return
536 BC	Foundation of the Temple is laid
500 BC	Temple is Finished
400 BC	End of Old Testament Era

950 900 850 800 750 700 650 600 550 500 450 400				
Egypt	Assyria		Babylon	Persia
N. & S. Kingdoms	Judah Alone		Exile	Post-Exile
△ Solomon dies	△ Israel falls	△ Judah falls		
			△ Captives return	
Major Prophets	Isaiah	Jeremiah/Lam.		
		Daniel		
		Ezekiel		
Minor Prophets Obadiah	Jonah Micah	Nahum		Haggai Malachi
Joel	Amos	Zephaniah		Zechariah
	Hosea	Habakkuk		
Other Prophets & OT Books Elijah				Esther
Elisha				Ezra
				Nehemiah

*https://www.biblequestions.org/bqar410.html

Our study will follow the Minor Prophets as they are shown in the above chart from left to right.

THE AUTHORS AND THE AUDIENCES

The Minor Prophets were active during a time of great political and social upheaval in the ancient Near East. Various empires were rising and falling. The Israelites were caught in the middle, often tempted to compromise their faith in order to survive.

Most of these prophetic works were written to address the spiritual abandonment of the Jews. This rejection often took the form of a disregard for the Law of Moses and the overt worship of idols to pagan gods.

Most of the books were addressed to the Southern Kingdom of Judah, some to the Northern Kingdom of Israel, and some to Gentile nations.

METHODS AND MAJOR THEMES

These books employ two primary forms of prophecy:

- Forthtelling: Informing the audience of their current spiritual condition in the eyes of God.
- Foretelling: Making predictions for their future.

Current language tends to think of "prophecy" as projecting the future. But Biblical prophets were typically more *Forthtellers* than *Foretellers*.

These two forms were used to communicate five reoccurring themes found throughout these writings:

1. **Sin** - Spiritual adultery in the form of idolatry, wickedness, and injustice.
2. **Call to Repent** - God's vengeance and pending judgment.
   A prophet's message was often in the form of *If this....then that.* Repent and things turn out better. Do not repent and the results will be ruinous.
3. **God's Forgiveness** - God's love and willingness to restore a relationship tainted by sin.
4. **Encouragement** – Inspiration to remain faithful and enjoy God's blessings.

A Long Walk with the Minor Prophets

5. **The coming Messiah** – The Assurance of a promised king.

MAJOR PROPHETS VS MINOR PROPHETS

The first 5 prophets in Biblical order are considered Major Prophets: Isaiah, Jeremiah, Lamentations, Ezekiel, Daniel. The remaining 12 books are Minor Prophets.

What distinguishes between a Major Prophet and a Minor Prophet?

- Were Major prophets of higher rank?
- Did Minor prophets preach in a "minor key"?
- Were Major prophets more important than Minor Prophets?

The answer is: *None of the Above*. The Major Prophets are called "Major" simply because the larger size of their writings. The Major Prophets provide sufficient Biblical materials for long studies of their own. In the Hebrew Bible, the "minor prophets" were called *The Book of the Twelve*, as it was originally a scroll that contained all twelve of these books.

RESOURCES

Beyond my four decades of personal preaching and teaching, several items were constructive in the development of this series of Bible studies.

Fortunately, my library included my hand-written notes from a 1980 college class in Old Testament Prophets. These papers were very useful during my preparation. Thanks to Dr. Don Garner, retired Professor of Old

A Long Walk with the Minor Prophets

Testament Studies, at Carson-Newman University for introducing me to so many insights.

Warren W. Wiersbe's "Be Series" of Bible book commentaries gave valuable explanation and elaboration on these texts.

Mary Cooney's *Journey with the Minor Prophets* provided useful historical and biblical background information.

The illustrated timelines found in the introductory words to most minor prophet studies originated at the following website: https://www.biblequestions.org/bqar410.html

JUST FOR FUN

On the day I was to teach on Obadiah, the first prophet in this series, I realized the words "Obadiah" and "Oklahoma" both begin with a long "O" sound and both have four syllables. I soon was singing the name "Obadiah" to the tune from the title song from Rogers and Hammerstein's musical *Oklahoma*. In a moment of inspiration, I quickly composed new lyrics to the familiar melody from this classic Broadway show. That evening, I closed the study of Obadiah with a light-hearted sing-along. Little did I know what I had started! The next week's lesson was on the prophet Joel. Therefore, I adapted a song written and performed by recording artist Billy Joel. Soon, other people in the study were writing clever lyrics about the minor prophets to go along with familiar melodies. Eventually we utilized karaoke soundtracks and even had closing *Karaoke Nights with the Minor Prophets* dedicated to singing all these songs as a method of reviewing our study.

Therefore, at the end of the closing lesson on each minor prophet in this book, you will find our lyrics to these parody songs. Enjoy them as a means of light-hearted fun and reexamination.

MESSAGES FOR CHRISTIANS

The books of the Major and Minor Prophets were written to predominately Jewish audiences over 2500 years ago. Many of their messages are echoed in the books of the New Testament written for Christians. For example, the Minor Prophets are quoted some 90 times in Revelation alone. Therefore, followers of Jesus can benefit from this study by getting to know God better and learning to live in a higher manner worthy of our calling.

So, join me on a long walk with these Minor Prophets. On the way we will discover a renewed appreciation for God's sovereignty, justice, mercy, and hope.

A Long Walk with the Minor Prophets

1 – OBADIAH
The Lost Book of the Bible

INTRODUCTION

My quick survey on Amazon.com found at least fifteen books with titles including the words "The Lost Books of the Bible." In a sense, the book of Obadiah is "The Lost Book INSIDE the Bible." In most copies of scripture, the entire content of Obadiah is contained on a single page. When I taught this study, I gave identical Bibles to seven volunteers. These people participated in an old fashioned "Bible Drill" or "Sword Drill" exercise. Awards were given to those who found the book of Obadiah in their Bible in the shortest amount of time.

While the brevity of Obadiah's words causes them to be elusive, there are significant messages here for God's people.

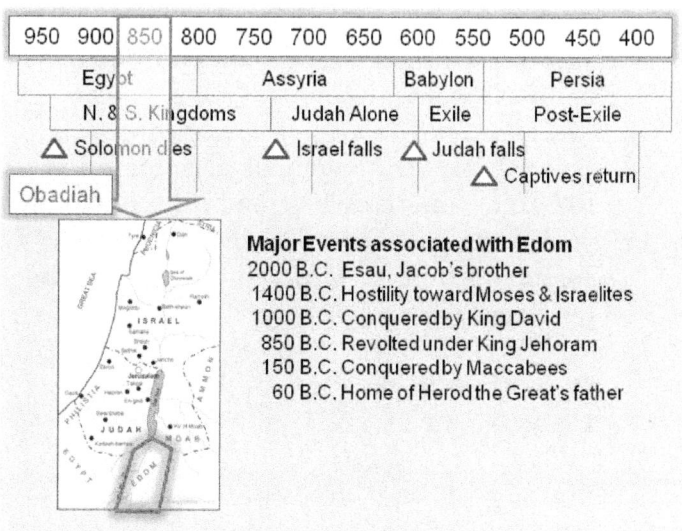

The Audience

Obadiah prophesized against Edom. The Edomites were the descendants of Esau, the brother of Jacob and son of Isaac and Rebecca who lived around 2000 B.C. The Edom was southwest of the Dead Sea.

So Esau (that is, Edom) settled in the hill country of Seir. Genesis 36:8 NIV

Today this land is part of the nation of Jordan. Some tourists in the Middle East have visited Edom without knowing it. The capital of Edom was Petra. I have traveled there a couple of times. This city, carved out of solid rock, is a fascinating place to experience. Petra was also featured in the motion picture *Indiana Jones and the Last Crusade*!

You can see by the points in the above timeline how Edom was controlled by Israel during and following the time of King David. But for most of Old Testament history, the Edomites lived independent of the Hebrews.

Because they had common ancestors in Isaac and Rebekah, the Israelites and the Edomites were distant cousins. For this reason, the law of Moses commanded the Jews to treat the Edomites respectfully.

Do not despise an Edomite, for the Edomites are related to you. Deuteronomy 23:7 NIV

But they still squabbled. In fact, theirs was a long-term family feud between the children of Jacob and the children of Esau. It began even when the twin boys were in Rebekah's womb:

22 The babies jostled each other within her, and she said, "Why is this happening to me?" So she went to inquire of the Lord.
23 The Lord said to her,
"Two nations are in your womb,
    and two peoples from within you will be separated;
one people will be stronger than the other,
    and the older will serve the younger." Genesis 25:22-23 NIV

The Lord Himself was prophetic in these words. Later, when the Hebrews were completing their forty years of wandering in the wilderness and headed toward the Promised Land, Moses asked Edom to allow them to pass through their land. Their request was abruptly rebuffed.

Then Edom came out against them with a large and powerful army. 21 Since Edom refused to let them go through their territory, Israel turned away from them. Numbers 20:20-21 NIV

Therefore, Obadiah addressed a contentious relationship with an extended history of friction and ill-will.

The Dates

The time of Obadiah's prophecy is uncertain. It clearly occurred following a season of severe and intense hostility from Edom toward the Hebrews. Scholars propose two primary possibilities:

- **In 850 BC**

    Edom's revolted under King Jehoram is recorded in 2 Kings 8.

    20 In the time of Jehoram, Edom rebelled against Judah and set up its own king. 21 So Jehoram went to Zair with all his chariots. The Edomites surrounded him and his chariot commanders, but he rose up and broke through by night; his army, however, fled back home. 22 To this day Edom has been in rebellion against Judah. 2 Kings 8:20-22a NIV

    Our study of the Minor Prophets places Obadiah following this event.

- **In 587 BC**

    Some historians think the destruction of Judah referred to by Obadiah took place when the Babylonians destroyed Jerusalem in 587 BC. There are some non-biblical records testifying Edom's participation in the fall of Jerusalem.

The Author:

The name Obadiah means *Servant* or *Worshiper of the Lord*. Beyond his name, the Bible does not reveal anything regarding this prophet. Obadiah was a common name in the Old Testament appearing some twenty times. Yet the prophet cannot be identified specifically with any of the other ten or eleven characters called by this name in the Bible.

The Uniqueness of the Book:

With only 21 verses in a single chapter, Obadiah is the shortest book in the Old Testament. Overall, Obadiah is the fourth shortest book in the Bible. Three New Testament books have fewer words: Philemon, 2nd John, and 3rd John.

THE MESSAGE OF OBEDIAH

The vision of Obadiah.
This is what the Sovereign Lord says about Edom—We have heard a message from the Lord:
  An envoy was sent to the nations to say,
"Rise, let us go against her for battle"— Obadiah 1 NIV

An ambassador was convincing leaders of neighboring nations to team up and go to battle against Edom. In the past, Edom cooperated with other nations against the Hebrews. Now the Edomites would be the target of a secret conspiracy. As you read Obadiah's words of judgment, emphasize the words *you and your* printed in bold type.

*All **your** allies will force **you** to the border;*
  ***your** friends will deceive and overpower **you**;*
*those who eat **your** bread will set a trap for **you**,*
  *but **you** will not detect it.* Obadiah 7 NIV

Former friends and allies would turn against them in destructive ways. What wrongs had they done in order to bring about such harsh action?

THE SINS OF EDOM

Obadiah focuses on at least three areas of unrighteousness on the part of the Edomites.

The Sin of Pride

The pride of your heart has deceived you,
  you who live in the clefts of the rocks
  and make your home on the heights,
you who say to yourself,
  'Who can bring me down to the ground?' Obadiah 3

The Edomites benefited from the peculiar geography of their land. It was a region of rugged mountains with high cliffs and narrow valleys. This dissuaded any invader from attacking. This also gave Edom a false sense of pride and security. But even entrenched evil is never totally secure.

Pride remains a problem today. People overconfidently say, *Oh, that will never happen to me.* I find intentionally placing myself among disadvantaged people helps keep my pride in check. For example, whenever I make pastoral visits to the skilled care area of a senior living facility, I am reminded these residents were once like me. They had healthy bodies and sound minds. This reflection grants me a humble perspective.

The Sin of Indifference

On the day you stood aloof
  while strangers carried off his wealth
and foreigners entered his gates
  and cast lots for Jerusalem,
  you were like one of them. Obadiah 11

When the Hebrews were falling and suffering, Edom failed to come to the aid of their distant cousins. This was a sin of omission. Rather than helping their relatives, they stood aloof.

Some municipalities have "bystander laws." These laws make it a crime for a person to not render assistance to a person in danger. This was the crime of the Edomites. They stood by while the Hebrews suffered.

The Sin of Gloating

You should not gloat over your brother
   in the day of his misfortune,
nor rejoice over the people of Judah
   in the day of their destruction,
nor boast so much
   in the day of their trouble.
13 You should not march through the gates of my people
   in the day of their disaster,
nor gloat over them in their calamity
   in the day of their disaster, Obadiah 12-13

Notice the two uses of the word "gloat" in these verses. It is bad enough to suffer. But to endure mocking while suffering creates an especially sharp sting.

Yes, the destruction the Hebrews experienced was due to their own disobedience and disregard of the Lord. STILL, this gloating was not permissible, especially toward their relatives. The Bible warns against rejoicing over the misfortunes of others.

Whoever mocks the poor shows contempt for their Maker;
   whoever gloats over disaster will not go unpunished.
Proverbs 17:5 NIV

One of the most severe penalties in football (and some other sports too) is *Taunting*! It is a penalty in God's book too.

THE RESPONSES OF GOD

The Echo Principle

The "Echo Principle" is a simple understanding: *What goes out tends to come back.* Consequences would fall upon the Edomites. Their hateful treatment of Judah would *echo* back to them.

As you have done, it will be done to you;
your deeds will return upon your own head. Obadiah 15

Smile and the world smiles with you. Grumble, and it grumbles back.

This principle is also found in other places in the Bible. Do you remember what happened to the Babylonian administrators who entrapped Daniel in order to throw him into the lion's den? THEY were thrown in the lion's den along with their wives and children (Daniel 6:24).

Paul describes the principle this way. *Do not be deceived, God is not mocked; for whatever a man sows, that he will also reap* (Galatians 6:7 NKJV). And in the Sermon on the Mount, Jesus said, *For in the same way you judge others, you will be judged, and with the measure you use, it will be measured to you* (Matthew 7:2 NIV).

I do not associate occurrences with *karma* or *fate* or *kismet*. Still, God created humans to be social beings.

We simply cannot survive unless we rely upon others. By God's design, when you relate with people honestly, considerately, and virtuously, they tend to respond to you in like manner. No wonder we are instructed to follow this "Golden Rule":

So in everything, do to others what you would have them do to you, for this sums up the Law and the Prophets. Matthew 7:12 NIV

Build your life with the finest of actions, and trust God to bring the appropriate replies back to you.

His Ultimate Triumph

The "Echo Principle" works with God too. The Lord declares He will be vindicated. For now, the Hebrews were down. But the story of Edom was not yet over.

Jacob will be a fire
*   and Joseph a flame;*
Esau will be stubble,
*   and they will set him on fire and destroy him.* Obadiah 18

"Jacob" referred to the southern kingdom of Judah and "Joseph" the northern kingdom of Israel. It was a reference to all the Hebrews. These two will be like "fire" and "flame." Esau, on the other hand, will be "stubble." By "stubble" Obadiah refers to the useless stem ends of herbs and especially cereal grasses remaining attached to the ground after harvest. The damage Esau brought upon the Hebrews will return upon them.

Just as you drank on my holy hill,

so all the nations will drink continually;
they will drink and drink
   and be as if they had never been. Obadiah 16 NIV

Around 300 BC, the Nabataean Arabs drove out the Edomites and occupied their key city of Petra. In time, Edom became a wasteland. Today, the capital city of Jerusalem is a thriving city and Petra is unoccupied and in ruins. In the end, God defeats His enemies and delivers His people.

Deliverers will go up on Mount Zion
   to govern the mountains of Esau.
And the kingdom will be the Lord's. Obadiah 21 NIV

As Christians, we believe that at a time of His own choosing, in this world or in the next, God will triumph over evil. All things wrong will be made right. When this occurs, everyone will recognize Jesus as the means to our salvation.

that at the name of Jesus every knee should bow,
   in heaven and on earth and under the earth,
11 and every tongue acknowledge that Jesus Christ is Lord,
   to the glory of God the Father. Philippians 2:10-11 NIV

ONE FINAL THOUGHT

One of the easier things about starting this series with Obadiah is the fact that his prophecies are directed toward "those people" in Edom rather than the Hebrews themselves. When we focus on what is wrong with <u>other</u> folks, we avoid looking inward at our own shortcomings. As we move ahead to other minor prophets, most of the words will be difficult messages addressed to God's own people.

A Long Walk with the Minor Prophets

OBADIAH by Jay McCluskey
Sung to the tune of *Oklahoma* by Rogers and Hammerstein.

O…ba-di-ah
He's the prophet with the tiny book
And he spoke God's call
To the kids of Esau
That their sins would have them on the hook

O…ba-di-ah
In their gloat, indifference, and pride
They were not so strong
To ignore their wrong
And an enemy would find their way inside!

Oh you know you didn't do what God said.
Now your bad deeds will fall on your head!

And God will say, NO!
You've done enough wrong
HEY! It's gone on too long
You're not doing fine, says Obadiah
Obadiah
O-B-A-D-I-(blank) A-H
Obadiah!

HEY!

A Long Walk with the Minor Prophets

A Long Walk with the Minor Prophets

2 - JOEL
Beware the Locust

What animal frightens you the most? Many people identify sharks, snakes, lions or bears as the most intimidating. But the animal that causes the most devastation in our world may surprise you. Spreading diseases like malaria, dengue, West Nile, yellow fever, Zika, chikungunya, and lymphatic filariasis, **the mosquito** kills more people than any other creature in the world. (Center for Disease Control, Article on their website dated August 17, 2023) We rarely think of insects as treacherous, even though they potentially are deadly. Joel prophesied in response to a calamity caused by an assailant almost as small as mosquitos: locusts.

INTRODUCTION

Historical Background

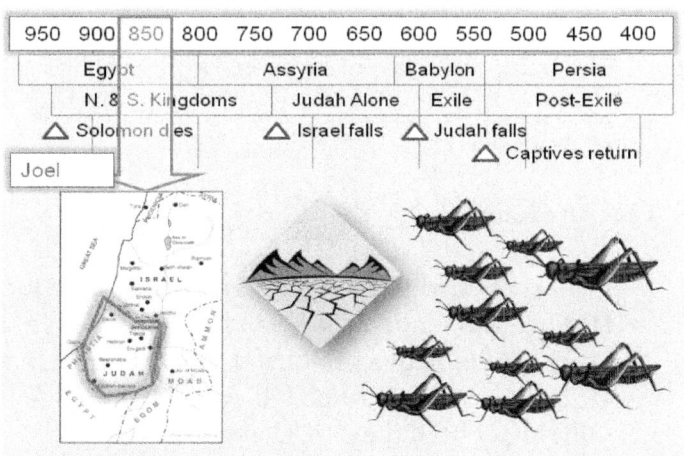

In Old Testament times, the economy of Canaan was based predominately on agriculture. Nature usually advocates for farmers, providing necessary sun and rain. But an agrarian economy can suffer hardship

29

from any number of natural disasters: droughts, livestock diseases, and insect infestations such as a locust invasion. The date of the book of Joel is uncertain. Some scholars believe it may have been written as early as 830 B.C.

The Author

The word of the Lord that came to Joel son of Pethuel. Joel 1:1 NIV

Joel's name blends the Bible's featured names for God: *Yahweh* and *Elohim*. Literally, the name says, *Yahweh Is Elohim*, or *The Lord is God*. "Joel" was a popular name. There actually are thirteen different characters in the Bible identified by the name "Joel." However, we know very little about the Prophet Joel other than his name and the name of his father, *Pethuel*. Joel's father's name means "open to God." It either could mean he was open-minded to God's leadership, or he was a spokesperson for God. Perhaps Joel was both a prophet and the son of a prophet.

The Audience

Joel prophesied to the Southern Kingdom of Judah. During this time, the Southern Kingdom was experiencing both a prolonged drought and a plague of locusts. As a result, there was considerable suffering of both the people and their livestock.

Joel's book educates people on what God says through the critical events they experience and how best to respond. The major themes of Joel are highlighted as we walk through the book.

LIFE IS HARD

Tell it to your children,
   and let your children tell it to their children,
   and their children to the next generation.
4 What the locust swarm has left
   the great locusts have eaten; Joel 1:3-4 NIV

Some events are so epic, their stories are passed along from generation to generation. My parents told me about their life as children during the Great Depression and World War 2. I told my children about watching the first landing on the moon. They will tell their children about the attacks of September 11 and the coronavirus pandemic.

Of course, in ancient times, storytelling was the primary method for recording significant occurrences. Long before print, broadcast, and digital communication, these tales were preserved through this means of oral tradition.

A cartoon showed a kangaroo with a baby kangaroo peeking out of the pouch. The caption read: *His mother determines his point of view.* This image reminds parents of their responsibility to teach the epic lessons they already learned to their children.

Joel compares the locust to an invading army with teeth like a lion.
   A nation has invaded my land,
      a mighty army without number;
   it has the teeth of a lion,
      the fangs of a lioness. Joel 1:6 NIV

A few verses later, Joel pointed his audience toward the devastation before them.

Despair, you farmers, wail, you vine growers;
grieve for the wheat and the barley,
because the harvest of the field is destroyed. Joel 1:11 NIV

Just within the previous few weeks of this writing, various corners of our world were struck by widespread fires, earthquakes, and floods. In such times, residents face the loss of so much of their lives and livelihoods. Judah's loss included the grains of wheat and barley as well as the grape harvest that produced wine.

Wake up, you drunkards, and weep!
Wail, all you drinkers of wine;
wail because of the new wine,
for it has been snatched from your lips. Joel 1:5 NIV

Notice drunkenness was the only specific sin associated by Joel with the locust plaque. Perhaps drunkards represented the careless people in the land. Most likely, Joel simply featured the vast extend of their agricultural loss.

People of faith must be reluctant to associate a natural disaster or health crisis with specific sins or with specific people. ONLY do this with a direct word from the Lord. Joel's point is valid: Life is Hard…FOR EVERYONE. Jesus said, *He* (God) *causes his sun to rise on the evil and the good, and sends rain on the righteous and the unrighteous* (Matthew 5:45b NIV). He also rejected the conclusion that people in his own day killed by a fallen tower were worse sinners than others (Luke 13:4).

IT CAN GET WORSE

On numerous occasions Joel mentions "the day of the Lord." This phrase refers to a coming day of God's apocalyptic judgment. The introduction of this study said the Minor Prophets were quoted 90 times in the book of Revelation. In Revelation waves of disasters fall as seals are broken, trumpets are played, and bowls are poured out. Notice how Joel and Revelation share much of the same intense imagery.

Blow the trumpet in Zion;
sound the alarm on my holy hill. Joel 2:1 NIV

> *Then the seven angels who had the seven trumpets prepared to sound them.* Revelation 8:6

Let all who live in the land tremble, for the day of the Lord is coming.
It is close at hand— 2 a day of darkness and gloom, a day of clouds and blackness. Joel 2:1b-2a NIV

> *When he opened the Abyss, smoke rose from it like the smoke from a gigantic furnace. The sun and sky were darkened by the smoke from the Abyss* Revelation 9:2 NIV

The Lord thunders at the head of his army; his forces are beyond number,
and mighty is the army that obeys his command. Joel 2:11a NIV

> *I saw heaven standing open and there before me was a white horse, whose rider is called Faithful and True* Revelation 19:11a NIV

Life is hard. Both Joel and Revelation reveal how life can get worse before it gets better.

THERE ARE APPROPRIATE RESPONSES

We easily take for granted the blessings from God until they are gone. The arrival of a calamity reminds us of our total dependence upon Him. During those times, Joel prescribes the following actions.

Mourn

Put on sackcloth, you priests, and mourn; wail, you who minister before the altar.
Come, spend the night in sackcloth, you who minister before my God;
for the grain offerings and drink offerings are withheld from the house of your God.
14 Declare a holy fast; call a sacred assembly.
Summon the elders and all who live in the land
to the house of the Lord your God, and cry out to the Lord. Joel 1:13-14 NIV

The palpable loss of life, health, and livelihood is real. Expressing grief and sorrow is fitting, appropriate, and healing in the aftermath of hurt.

Repent

"Even now," declares the Lord,
  "return to me with all your heart,
  with fasting and weeping and mourning."

13 Rend your heart and not your garments.
Return to the Lord your God, for he is gracious and compassionate,
slow to anger and abounding in love,
  and he relents from sending calamity. Joel 2:12-13 NIV

Joel called for inward (*rend your heart*) as well as outward expressions (*rend your garments*) of repentance. Do not simply go through the motions of remorse. Let it be genuine and authentic.

THERE IS A GRACIOUS DELIVERANCE

Eventually, Joel told the people to stop looking around at the devastation and to start looking ahead toward God's healing.

Then the Lord was jealous for his land
  and took pity on his people.
19 The Lord replied to them:
"I am sending you grain, new wine and olive oil,
  enough to satisfy you fully;
never again will I make you
  an object of scorn to the nations.
20 "I will drive the northern horde far from you,
  pushing it into a parched and barren land;
And its stench will go up; its smell will rise." Joel 2:18-20 NIV

It could have been even worse. The *northern horde* may refer to the locust. More likely it was a prophecy of the Assyrians under the leadership of Sennacharib. They defeated the northern kingdom of Israel in 722 BC and were on the cusp of taking down Judah in 701 BC. But in one night 185,000 of Sennacharib's soldiers died and he retreated from Jerusalem (2 Kings 19:35-36). The prophecy spoke this truth: 185,000 decaying bodies would create a great stench.

Not only does God's deliverance take the form of rescue for God's people, Joel also promised God's restoration.

I will repay you for the years the locusts have eaten—

> *the great locust and the young locust,*
> *the other locusts and the locust swarm—*
> *my great army that I sent among you.*
> *26 You will have plenty to eat, until you are full,*
> *and you will praise the name of the Lord your God,*
> *who has worked wonders for you;* Joel 2:25-26 NIV

The person in a right relationship with God will be restored more than before. God IS a God of healing and restoration. If you have been sick, you got better. Often, life gets better in this world. But even when it does not, we are confident in the complete deliverance of eternal life.

THE BEST IS YET TO BE

Joel declares their time of trouble is followed by a time of triumph and glory.

Sometimes God's planned blessings are in this world but in the distant future.

The best-known words from Joel are found in the second chapter.

> *"And afterward, I will pour out my Spirit on all people.*
> *Your sons and daughters will prophesy,*
>   *your old men will dream dreams,*
>   *your young men will see visions.* Joel 2:28 NIV

We know this verse because Peter saw a correlation when he quoted it in Acts 2 on the Day of Pentecost. Remember, the Holy Spirit empowered Peter and the disciples about 800 years after Joel's time. God made promises through Joel He did not fulfill until centuries later. In troubled times remember: God's plan IS always advancing.

Sometimes God's planned blessings are in the heavenly world.

"In that day the mountains will drip new wine,
 and the hills will flow with milk;
all the ravines of Judah will run with water.
A fountain will flow out of the Lord's house Joel 3:18 NIV

It is an idyllic picture of Judah and the temple. Over the centuries, the land of Israel has been ravaged by wars, famines, droughts, and invasions of insects. But a day is coming when the land will be like the garden of Eden. Joel's description matches well with the vision of the New Jerusalem in Revelation 22:

Then the angel showed me the river of the water of life, as clear as crystal, flowing from the throne of God and of the Lamb 2 down the middle of the great street of the city. On each side of the river stood the tree of life, bearing twelve crops of fruit, yielding its fruit every month. And the leaves of the tree are for the healing of the nations Revelation 22:1-2 NIV

Jerusalem is the only city of antiquity that was not built near a great river. The Egyptians had the Nile. The Babylonians had the Tigress and Euphrates. Rome had the Tiber. But in His eternal kingdom, Jerusalem will have a life-giving river that proceeds from the very throne of God.

CONCLUSION

The Lord dwells in Zion! Joel 3:21b

A Long Walk with the Minor Prophets

What a wonderful phrase to close this book! Joel's prophecies began with tragedy and closed with the triumphant reign of the Lord. In all this, the Lord never left. He is the true Immanuel, the God who is with us. Matthew's gospel concludes with the same promise from the resurrected Jesus: *I am with you always* (Matthew 28:20).

LESSONS FOR CHRISTIANS

Physical Hardships Should Remind Us of God and Encourage Us to Draw Closer to Him

The devastation of the locust was more than a physical phenomenon. It was a spiritual revelation of the power of God's judgment and the necessity of faith. When difficulties occur, some may walk away from God. The wise will walk toward Him.

God Provides Blessings for Those Who Remain Faithful to Him

Be faithful, even to the point of death, and I will give you life as your victor's crown (Revelation 2:10b). Yes, it is easier to have faith when life is easy. But even when life is hard, even when you do not understand the pain you are going through, lean into the Lord and not away from Him.

The Ultimate "Day of The Lord" Still Awaits

42 "Therefore keep watch, because you do not know on what day your Lord will come. 43 But understand this: If the owner of the house had known at what time of night the thief was coming, he would have kept watch and would not have let his house be broken into. 44 So you also must be ready, because the

Son of Man will come at an hour when you do not expect him.
Matthew 24:42-44 NIV

God will have the last word. So be ready.

LOCUST PLAGUE by Jay McCluskey
Sung to the tune of *Uptown Girl* by Billy Joel.

Locust Plague
You came through and now our plants are dead
Ate them all with your lion-like teeth
Now there's nothing left for us to eat.

It's all because of a Locust Plague
You point us to the things the Lord has said
Now in response we will repent and mourn
And wait until you play that trumpet horn.

And when things get worse
We won't curse, run, or deplore.
Cause when the time comes
Our great God He will restore

From a Locust Plague
Day of the Lord is only just ahead
Joel says the best is yet to be
Perhaps on earth or in eternity.

That's why we're free from a locust plague.

3 – JONAH
Chapters 1-2
The Runaway Prophet

Jonah is the best known of the Minor Prophets. This is in part because it is written in the form of a narrative rather than a collection of oracles like most of the other Minor Prophets. It also is quite an amazing story. We teach our children about Jonah because it includes a boat and the adventure of a ride inside a giant fish. While the fish gets all the attention, this is far more than a fish story.

- The fish is mentioned four times
- Nineveh is mentioned nine times
- Jonah is mentioned eighteen times
- God is mentioned thirty-eight times.

One of the most interesting books in scripture actually is a tale of God's love for the world, His plan to reach the world, and a man's hesitance to be part of this plan.

INTRODUCTION

Author

> Jonah is unique because he is mentioned in the Old Testament in a place other than the book bearing his name:

> *He (King Jeroboam II of Israel) was the one who restored the boundaries of Israel from Lebo Hamath to the Dead Sea, in accordance with the word of the Lord, the God of Israel, spoken through his servant Jonah son of Amittai, the prophet from Gath Hepher.* 2 Kings 14:25 NIV

A Long Walk with the Minor Prophets

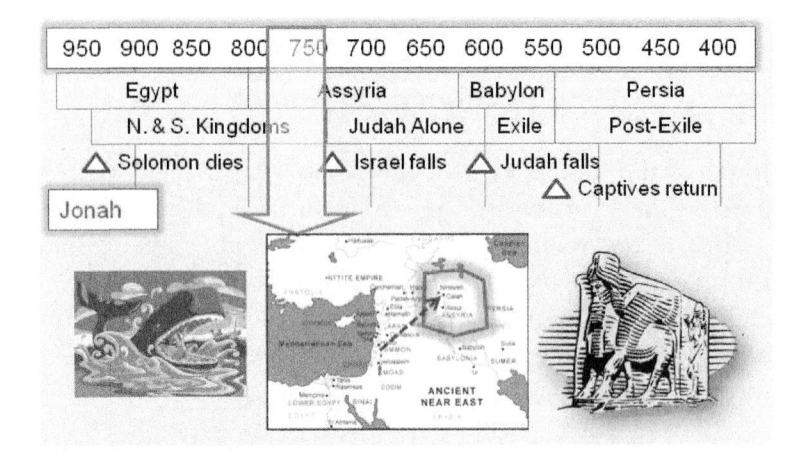

Jonah's name means "dove." Ironically a dove often is associated with peace. However, there is little about Jonah's story that can be called "peaceful." The mention of Jonah's father both in 2 Kings and in the opening verse of the book of Jonah affirms these are the same person. Jonah's father's name, Amittai, means "truth." A Jewish tradition says Jonah was the son of the widow of Zarephath. While this relationship is not mentioned in scripture, if true, Jonah's life would be marked with both the trauma of being swallowed by a fish AND being raised from the dead by Elijah (1 Kings 17).

Historical Background

The reference to Jereboam II in 2 Kings 14 gives a timestamp to Jonah's story. Jereboam II's reign was around 770 BC (about 160 years after Solomon's death). Jonah is the first prophet in our studies to reside in the northern kingdom of Israel.

Internationally, Assyrian was a growing empire northeast from Canaan (see the map on the graphic).

Nineveh was the capital city of Assyria. Their threat to Israel created a strong animosity from the Hebrews toward the Ninevites.

This study covers the first two chapters of Jonah's story. Each section will feature a key word description and a bit of a rhyme.

REBELLION: GOD SAYS "GO." JONAH SAYS "NO!"

The word of the Lord came to Jonah son of Amittai: Go to the great city of Nineveh and preach against it, because its wickedness has come up before me. Jonah 1:1 NIV

God gave Jonah a mission to rebuke the Assyrians for their wickedness and threaten them with destruction if they did not repent. Instead, Jonah went the opposite direction.

But Jonah ran away from the Lord and headed for Tarshish. He went down to Joppa, where he found a ship bound for that port. After paying the fare, he went aboard and sailed for Tarshish to flee from the Lord. Jonah 1:3 NIV

Joppa was a long way from Jonah's hometown. Gath Hepher (2 Kings 14:25) was about three miles northeast of Nazareth. It is often noted that Tarshish was in the opposite direction from Nineveh. This is true when sailing the Mediterranean Sea. But Jonah <u>already</u> headed away from Nineveh even on his land journey to Joppa.

Jonah possessed an opposing attitude to this will of God. Honestly, Jonah preferred Nineveh be destroyed. He had no desire to go to Israel's enemy and give them the opportunity to repent. This in spite of the fact <u>*The word of the Lord*</u> (verse 1) had come to Jonah.

Obeying the will of God should be a priority for every follower of the Lord, even when He calls us to do something we prefer not to do. Jonah needed to remember the will of God is the expression of the love of God. God loved Jonah. God loved the Israelites. God loved Ninevites. Jesus taught His disciples to love in this higher way:

> *You have heard that it was said, "Love your neighbor and hate your enemy. But I tell you, love your enemies and pray for those who persecute you, that you may be children of your Father in heaven.* Matthew 5:43-45a NIV

Instead, Jonah became a runaway prophet. He was ready to quit. At one time or another during their ministries, Moses, Elijah, and Jeremiah felt like giving up too. But God would not let them.

Where is your "Nineveh?" How do you respond when God asks you to do something you honestly do not want to do? Do you run away? Do you make excuses? Popular false teachings say things like *Follow your heart* and *Be true to yourself*. But Jesus said *Follow me* and *Whoever wants to be my disciple must deny himself*.

Throughout the Bible God gives two commands: To everyone He says, *Come to Me*. To His people He says: *Go into the world*. God bestows a missionary vocation upon all His followers.

In the late 1800's a British composer named H. Ernest Nichol penned a hymn I remember from my childhood:

We've a story to tell to the nations that will set their hearts to the right.

This was Jonah's calling and ours. If we will tell God's story to the people, it has the power to transform their hearts to righteousness.

REGRET: JONAH SAYS "NO." OTHERS SAY "WOE."

Then the Lord hurled a violent wind on the sea, and such a violent storm arose on the sea that the ship threatened to break apart. 1:4 HCSB

In response to Jonah's desertion, God caused a great storm to break loose over the water. The verb *hurled* is the same word of Saul throwing a javelin at David (1 Samuel 19:10-12). But Jonah did not carry the cost of his disobedience alone. The sailors onboard also paid a price. Not only were their lives threatened, but the economic gains of their journey were thrown into the sea.

All the sailors were afraid and each cried out to his own god. And they threw the cargo into the sea to lighten the ship. But Jonah had gone below deck, where he lay down and fell into a deep sleep. Jonah 1:5 NIV

Jonah brought trouble to a boatload of pagan sailors because he fled. Rather than being the blessing God desired, Jonah was a curse to the men on the ship with him. Such is the nature of sin. Innocent people routinely pay for the mistakes made by others.

Joshua 7 tells the story of a man named Achan. He disobeyed God's instructions and kept some of the bounty from Joshua's defeat of Jericho. In response, thirty-six Hebrew soldiers fell in their next battle. These kind of stories cause us to ask, *How much is my sin costing others?*

REPENT: GOD SHOWS GRACE. JONAH REPENTS IN HASTE.

A casting of lots identified Jonah as the cause of the storm. The sailors initially rejected Jonah's offer to be thrown overboard and instead worked harder to save the ship. When they finally did toss Jonah into the water, they asked Jonah's God for forgiveness.

15 They took Jonah and threw him overboard, and the raging sea grew calm. 16 At this the men greatly feared the Lord, and they offered a sacrifice to the Lord and made vows to him. Jonah 1:15-16 NIV

At this point, the sailors appear more righteous than the prophet! No doubt, Jonah expected to die in the waters of the sea. But when he woke up inside the fish, he realized God graciously spared him.

Now the Lord provided a huge fish to swallow Jonah, and Jonah was in the belly of the fish three days and three nights. Jonah 1:17 NIV

The poetic section of Jonah occurs in chapter two as Jonah prayed from inside the belly of the fish. God did a miraculous thing in sparing Jonah's life. Now, instead of running from the Lord, Jonah demonstrated how to turn to the Lord both in attitude and in action.

Pray for God's Help

Jonah prayed to the Lord his God from inside the fish: In my distress I called to the Lord, and He answered me. Jonah 2:1-2a NIV

Some prayers are *prayers of affection* where we recognize the pleasant blessings the Lord grants to us. Some prayers are *prayers of affliction* when we are amid a calamity brought on by our own rebellion. Jonah prayed here because he was in danger, not because he delighted in the Lord. Still, it is better to pray with a lesser motivation than to not pray at all.

Most of what Jonah prayed is from the Psalms. Certainly, he was thankful he knew some scripture to pray. Athanasius the church father said it well:

- *Most of scripture speaks to us, but the Psalms speak for us.*

Accept God's Discipline

Jonah realized it was God who caused him to be in the sea.

*You hurled me into the depths, into the very heart of the seas,
    And the currents swirled about me;
All your waves and breakers swept over me.* Jonah 2:3 NIV

The fact God chastened His servant is proof Jonah was truly a child of God. The author of Hebrews wrote, *For the Lord disciplines those he loves, and he punishes each one he accepts as his child.* Hebrews 12:6 NLT.

Jonah could agree with the words of the Psalm:

> *The Lord has chastened me severely, but He has not given me over to death.* Psalm 118:18 NKJV

Yield to God's Will

> *I will fulfill what I have vowed. Salvation is from the Lord!* Jonah 2:9 NIV

For Jonah there was no more running. Jonah could not save himself. No one on earth could save him. **But God could** because *salvation is of the Lord.* Jonah 2:9 NKJV

As terrible as it was for Jonah inside a fish, it was not as bad as living in rebellion from the Lord.

RETURN – THE FISH SAYS *OUT WITH YOU.* JESUS GIVES A FORESHADOWING CLUE

> *And the Lord commanded the fish, and it vomited Jonah onto dry land.* Jonah 2:10 NIV

You do not always get an opportunity to right a wrong. But Jonah did. You do not always get a second chance: But Jonah did. In a famous section of William Shakespeare's drama, *Julius Caesar,* Brutus urges Cassius to enter battle with Octavius and Anthony. Brutus advocates that a missed opportunity will be lost forever.

> *"There is a tide in the affairs of men*
> *Which, taken at the flood, leads on to fortune;*
> *Omitted, all the voyage of their life*
> *Is bound in shallows and in miseries.*
> *On such a full sea are we now afloat;*
> *And we must take the current when it serves,*
> *Or lose our ventures."*

With due respect to Shakespeare, Jonah did NOT lose the opportunity for his *venture*.

Centuries after this story occurred, Jonah became a sign pointing to the power and identity of Jesus. When skeptics asked Jesus for a sign, He gave this reply.

He answered, "A wicked and adulterous generation asks for a sign! But none will be given it except the sign of the prophet Jonah. For as Jonah was three days and three nights in the belly of a huge fish, so the Son of Man will be three days and three nights in the heart of the earth." Matthew 12:39-40 NIV

Jesus repeats this teaching in Matthew 16:4. It also appears in Luke 11:29.

Free from the big fish, Jonah also was free to obey the Lord and to take God's message to Nineveh. But as we will see in our next study, Jonah still had lessons to learn. God prepares mission fields for His people. But the Lord also performs the equally challenging task of preparing His missionaries to go and serve. All this reflects God's devotion toward changing lives.

- *The company of Jesus is not people streaming to a shrine; and it is not people making up an audience for a speaker; it is laborers engaged in the harvesting task of reaching their perplexed and seeking brethren with something so vital that, if it is received, it will change their lives.* -Elton Trueblood, *The Company of the Committed.*

A Long Walk with the Minor Prophets

A Long Walk with the Minor Prophets

4 – JONAH
Chapters 3-4
The Resentful Prophet

At the end of Jonah 2, the great fish deposited Jonah onto dry land. That moment leads up to ponder an old question:

Was the great fish more relieved to be rid of Jonah or was Jonah more relieved to be rid of the great fish?

As in our first study on Jonah 1 and 2, we will walk through the final two chapters of the story. We are focusing on words which begin with the letter "R."

RECOMMISSION

Occasionally, a change is so dramatic, a *recommission* is in order. When a ship receives a major re-fitting, it may be *recommissioned*. It may even receive a new name and purpose. It is not the same anymore. A sanctuary with major renovations may be *re-dedicated*. Jonah 3 opens with the prophet's *recommissioning* as a missionary to Nineveh.

Notice how three verses of Jonah's *recommission* in chapter 3 compare with his first commission in chapter 1.

Then the word of the Lord came to Jonah a second time: 2 "Go to the great city of Nineveh and proclaim to it the message I give you." Jonah 3:1-2 NIV

The word of the Lord came to Jonah son of Amittai: 2 "Go to the great city of Nineveh and preach against it, because its wickedness has come up before me." Jonah 1:1-2

In his *recommission* God promised to give Jonah the exact message to declare. Perhaps this was more reassuring to Jonah than the original order to simply *preach against* the great city. But the key phrase is that God's word came *a second time.* A statistic in basketball is "second chance points." This accumulates when a team fails on its first shot but manages to get the rebound and then score. Jonah received a "second chance" to fulfill his calling to the Ninevites.

Some items may be "recommissioned" with a new purpose. An old pot can become a planter. If you cut off the bottom of a milk jug, it becomes a scoop. I remember seeing a tuba that was transformed into a lampstand. But Jonah received the **exact same purpose**: *Go preach to Nineveh.* Matthew's gospel concludes with what Christians call "The Great Commission." To every new generation of Christians, we receive "The Great Re-Commission" to fulfill the same purpose of teaching all nations.

RESPONSE

Chapter three is all about responses or reactions.

Jonah's Response

In contrast to his Rebellion in Chapter 1 and Repenting in Chapter 2, Jonah obeyed by going to the city and delivering God's message.

Jonah obeyed the word of the Lord and went to Nineveh. Now Nineveh was a very large city; it took three days to go through it. Jonah 2:3 NIV

As the capital city of the Assyrian Empire, Nineveh dominated the ancient Near East for most of 900 to 612 BC. It was founded in ancient times by Noah's great-grandson, Nimrod (Genesis 10:11). Four times in this book, Nineveh is called a "great city."

The preposition *through* in Jonah 2:3 could be in reference to the circumference rather than the diameter of the city. Either way, the sheer size of the city was impressive. It is reported that Nineveh's walls were 50 feet high and wide enough for three chariots to ride abreast. (The ruins of ancient Nineveh are located in modern day Iraq. Photos of the area can be found on the internet.)

Nineveh not only was great in its dimensions, it also was great in sin. The Assyrians were known for their violence and lack of mercy. In 722 BC, when Assyria eventually defeated the kingdom of Israel, its ten tribes disappeared in history. Nineveh's rough reputation probably contributed to Jonah's hesitation to go there.

When Jonah arrived in the city, he preached the message God gave him:

And Jonah began to enter into the city a day's journey, and he cried, and said, Yet forty days, and Nineveh shall be overthrown. Jonah 3:4 NIV

Forty days is a familiar timeline for some of the Bible's significant events:

- It rained on Noah's Ark 40 days (Genesis 7:12)
- Moses stayed on Mt. Sinai for 40 days (Exodus 24:18)

- The 12 Spies studied the Promise Land 40 days (Numbers 13:25)
- Goliath taunted the Hebrew army for 40 days (1 Samuel 17:16)
- Elijah traveled 40 days to Mt. Horeb (1 Kings 19:8)
- Jesus tempted 40 days in the wilderness (Matthew 4:2)
- Resurrected Jesus appeared 40 days before His ascension (Acts 1:3)

Consisting of only eight words in English and only five words in Hebrew, Jonah's message was simple, straightforward, direct, bold, and blunt. One may hold that such a brash and confrontive method would not be effective. But remarkably, it worked!

The Ninevites' Response

So the people of Nineveh believed God, and proclaimed a fast, and put on sackcloth, from the greatest of them even to the least of them. Jonah 3:5 NIV

From the least to the greatest, Jonah's message created the desired effect: the people repented! Jonah feared the Ninevites would kill him. Instead, they believed him! Even the king issued a decree for everyone to fast and pray in the hope that God would not bring destruction upon them (Jonah 3:6-9).

Despite Jonah's rebellion and reluctance, the Lord used Jonah effectively. He got past his past! You do not have to read far into the Bible to find the trend of God forgiving His servants and restoring them to effective ministry.

- Moses killed a man.
- David had an affair.
- Peter denied Jesus three times.

The simple truth is that transformation always is God's work far more than it is our own. One of my favorite adages says, *God hits mighty licks with crooked sticks!*

Perhaps Jonah's skin was bleached by the fish's gastric juices. Did he look so peculiar that it got people's attention and they considered his message more seriously? If so, the Bible does not say. But more important than how the Ninevites saw Jonah is the fact that they saw and responded to the Lord.

Centuries later, Jesus affirmed the response of the citizens of Nineveh in contrast to the people in His own day who refused to believe in Him.

The men of Nineveh will stand up at the judgment with this generation and condemn it; for they repented at the preaching of Jonah, and now something greater than Jonah is here. Matthew 12:41 NIV

God's Response

When God saw what they did and how they turned from their evil ways, he relented and did not bring on them the destruction he had threatened. Jonah 3:10 NIV

The King James Version says God *repented.* But *relented* is the better translation. The Lord changed

His course. It is God's nature to *relent* and *forgive*. He had done that for Jonah. Now he did the same for the Ninevites.

Some Old Testament scholars and historians observe that (for a season), the Assyrians became less aggressive and more peaceful after the ministry of Jonah.

RESENTFUL

If this book had ended at the last verse of chapter 3, history would remember Jonah as one of the greatest of the prophets. But rather than feel successful, Jonah felt resentful. He was mad at God for acting like God!

But to Jonah this seemed very wrong, and he became angry. 2 He prayed to the Lord, "Isn't this what I said, Lord, when I was still at home? That is what I tried to forestall by fleeing to Tarshish. I knew that you are a gracious and compassionate God, slow to anger and abounding in love, a God who relents from sending calamity. 3 Now, Lord, take away my life, for it is better for me to die than to live." Jonah 4:1-3 NIV

For the second time in this account Jonah prayed. He prayed the best prayer in the worst place: inside the great fish. Here he prayed the worst prayer in the best place: the city where God showed mercy.

In his commentary, Warren Wiersbe makes an interesting comparison between Jonah and the two brothers in Jesus' parable of The Prodigal Son. Before, Jonah was like the younger son running away from his father in rebellion. Now, he was like the older brother sulking because mercy was given.

Jonah was a good theologian and knew God's heart was compassionate. Now he was angry. Perhaps Jonah was upset about potential damage to his reputation. Remember, the test of a true prophet was whether or not his prophecies materialized:

If what a prophet proclaims in the name of the LORD does not take place or come true, that is a message the LORD has not spoken. That prophet has spoken presumptuously. Do not be afraid of him. Deuteronomy 18:22 NIV

While most prophecies had no exact timeline, Jonah's prophecy against Nineveh did: Forty Days! When Jonah returned to Israel, would he be thought of as a "false prophet" because Nineveh was not destroyed?

In reply, the Lord challenged Jonah regarding his attitude: *But the Lord replied, "Is it right for you to be angry?"* Jonah 4:4 NIV

God rescued the Ninevites. Nineveh was no longer a mission field, but Jonah was. Now the Lord tried to rescue Jonah, providing a simple plant as an object lesson.

5 Jonah had gone out and sat down at a place east of the city. There he made himself a shelter, sat in its shade and waited to see what would happen to the city. 6 Then the Lord God provided a leafy plant and made it grow up over Jonah to give shade for his head to ease his discomfort, and Jonah was very happy about the plant. 7 But at dawn the next day God provided a worm, which chewed the plant so that it withered. 8 When the sun rose, God provided a scorching east wind, and the sun blazed on Jonah's head so that he grew faint. He wanted to die,

A Long Walk with the Minor Prophets

and said, "It would be better for me to die than to live." Jonah 4:5-8 NIV

Jonah was angry that Nineveh was spared. But he also was upset that a plant died. The Lord, the other hand, looked at the city with pity and compassion.

10 But the Lord said, "You have been concerned about this plant, though you did not tend it or make it grow. It sprang up overnight and died overnight. 11 And should I not have concern for the great city of Nineveh, in which there are more than a hundred and twenty thousand people who cannot tell their right hand from their left—and also many animals?" Jonah 4:10-11 NIV

This number of children provides an indication of Nineveh's population. If preschoolers numbered 120,000, the total population was possibly as high as one million people.

The legendary country music singer Hank Williams crooned a question in his signature song:

- *Why can't I free your doubtful mind and melt your cold, cold, heart?*

God tried to melt Jonah's cold, cold, heart. The prophet's heart was "heart-less."

In the book of Jonah, God gets the first word and the last word. The story is unique in that it ends in a question. We are not told what happened to Jonah. The fact that Jonah himself was the only one who could write the story may indicate he eventually saw things God's way. After all, he too was a great recipient of God's compassionate grace.

A Long Walk with the Minor Prophets

While we cannot answer the question for Jonah, we can answer for ourselves. Will we reflect and celebrate God's compassion? Will we embrace a missionary spirit affirming God's desire for all the world's nations and nationalities to respond to Him? Decide now and write the ending to your story.

A Long Walk with the Minor Prophets

JONAH by Roni Starr
To the tune of Dolly Parton's *Jolene*.

Jonah, Jonah, Jonah, Jonah,
It's time to go evangelize the land.
Jonah, Jonah, Jonah, Jonah,
Repent and know God's mercy is at hand.

Tarshish was much better than,
Following God's almighty plan,
Because the enemy lived in Nineveh,
Soon he thought he'd get his wish,
But he spent three nights in a fish,
Because God had other plans for Jonah.

After praying in distress,
Admitting he had made a mess,
God heard the grateful prayer of Jonah.
Vomited up on dry land,
It was time to share God's future plans,
Through the mighty preaching of Jonah.

Jonah, Jonah, Jonah, Jonah,
It's time to go evangelize the land.
Jonah, Jonah, Jonah, Jonah,
Repent and know God's mercy is at hand.

The king of Nineveh prayed,
And the people turned from their evil ways,
But God's mercy wasn't fair to Jonah,
He cared so much for a plant,
And learned just why God would grant,
Forgiveness for His people and Jonah.

Jonah, Jonah, Jonah, Jonah,
It's time to go evangelize the land.

A Long Walk with the Minor Prophets

Jonah, Jonah, Jonah, Jonah,
Repent and know God's mercy is at hand.

A Long Walk with the Minor Prophets

5 – AMOS
Chapters 1 - 2
Judgment to All

Is it true that obedience to God's rules brings blessings to lives? Yes!
Is it also true that disobedience to God's rules brings hardship? Yes.

Indeed. These are truths we affirm in faith. But can we also say the converse is true?

If someone's life is going favorably, does that mean they are in God's will? Not necessarily.
If someone is suffering, does that mean they are out of God's will? Not at all.

Because things were going well for them in the northern Kingdom of Israel, the citizens assumed they were living obedient lives. They thought: *God is certainly on our side!* Thus, the citizens possessed a spirit of overconfident nationalism. They expected the *Day of the Lord* would soon strike down all their enemies and establish Israel as the undisputed ruler of the region. However, when you presume God's favor is on your side, you can readily neglect Him and cease living in ways that honor Him.

INTRODUCTION

Amos lived in a time when society appeared to be changing radically for the good.

- The northern kingdom of Israel reached its greatest heights in the first half of the 8th century BC.

- Both Israel and Judah were at peace with their neighbors.

A Long Walk with the Minor Prophets

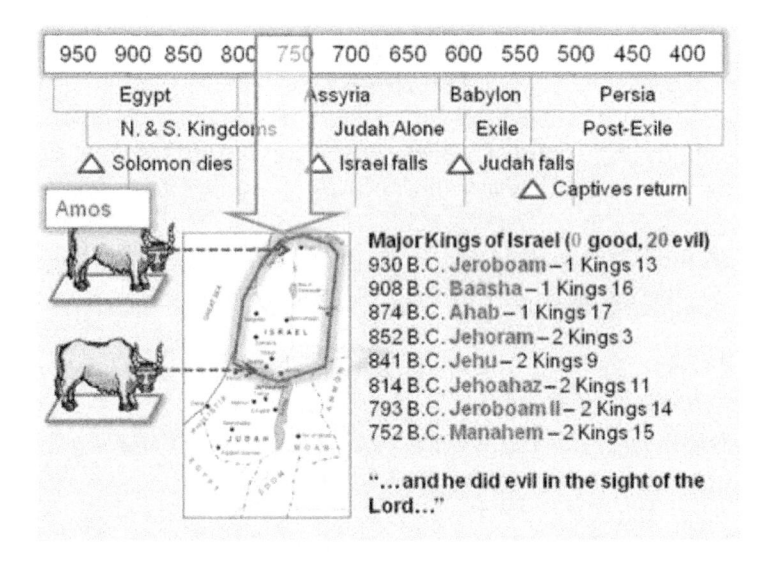

950 900 850 800	750	700 650 600 550 500 450 400
Egypt		Assyria	Babylon	Persia
N. & S. Kingdoms		Judah Alone	Exile	Post-Exile
△ Solomon dies		△ Israel falls △ Judah falls
		△ Captives return

Amos

Major Kings of Israel (0 good, 20 evil)
930 B.C. Jeroboam – 1 Kings 13
908 B.C. Baasha – 1 Kings 16
874 B.C. Ahab – 1 Kings 17
852 B.C. Jehoram – 2 Kings 3
841 B.C. Jehu – 2 Kings 9
814 B.C. Jehoahaz – 2 Kings 11
793 B.C. Jeroboam II – 2 Kings 14
752 B.C. Manahem – 2 Kings 15

"...and he did evil in the sight of the Lord..."

Because less money had to be invested in military defense, there were more funds to go to the general economy. Israel was located along major trade routes. Therefore, peacetime increased commerce and profitability.

But, to adapt the words to the familiar hymn, behind all this peace and prosperity, it was not "well with their souls." There were many ills around and it fell to a common farmer named Amos to name them.

When studying the first two chapters of Amos, it is helpful to follow the map at the end of this chapter. Notice how surrounding nations are addressed first. Amos is like an archer with a quiver of eight prophetic arrows of judgment fire to shoot.

JUDGMENT ON THE NEIGHBORS OF THE HEBREWS

The launch of each of these eight prophecies began with the same declaration:

For three transgressions and for four, I will not relent....

The phrase, *For three transgressions and for four,* was a poetic reference meaning an indefinite number has finally come to an end. In our vernacular we may say, *I'm down to my last nerve.* But how many "nerves" go by before only this last one remains? When we say, *That is the last straw,* how many "straws" are gone to reach this last one? THAT is an indefinite number that has finally come to an end.

The first six judgments fall on six of the Hebrew's closest neighbors.

Damascus (Syria) –

Amos first called out Syria and its capital, Damascus.

Their Sin:

Because she threshed Gilead with sledges having iron teeth, Amos 1:3b NIV

Some Hebrews lived in Gilead, east of the Jordan River. The Syrians were inhumane to them, *threshing* through them like they were nothing but stalks of grain.

Their Judgment:

I will send fire Amos 1:4 (Repeated in verses 7, 10, 12, 14)

This phrase means *I will send judgment*. In these verses "fire" represented the holiness and judgment of God.

I will send fire on the house of Hazael that will consume the fortresses of Ben-Hadad.
5 I will break down the gate of Damascus; I will destroy the king who is in the Valley of Aven and the one who holds the scepter in Beth Eden.
The people of Aram will go into exile to Kir," says the Lord. Amos 1:4-5 NIV

Their days were numbered. Though defeated in several battles by the Hebrews, Syria ultimately fell to the Assyrians. Later, the land came under the dominion of the Babylonian, Persian, Greek, and Roman empires.

Gaza / Philistia

The Philistines occupied five key cities along the southwest coast of Palestine (Joshua 13:3). The biblical stories of Samson and Goliath report the hostile history between the Hebrews and the Philistines.

Their Sin:

Because she took captive whole communities and sold them to Edom, Amos 1:6b NIV

The Philistines traded in human lives. They raided Jewish villages and captured people to be sold as slaves. The Law of Moses allowed slavery as a type of "lifeline" for a person in desperate circumstances. It also provided for the release of slaves.

The Philistines captured people against their will and sold them like cattle. To make matters worse, the Philistines sold these slaves to Israel's ancient enemy, the Edomites. We featured these distant relatives of the Hebrews in our study of Obadiah. They were descendants of Esau. It was a case of brother enslaving brother.

Their Judgment:

I will send fire on the walls of Gaza Amos 1:7a NIV
I will turn my hand against Ekron, till the last of the Philistines are dead," Amos 1:8b NIV

Again, God's judgment was intense like fire. While weakened by the rise of the Assyrian Empire, the Philistines were defeated and exiled under Nebuchadnezzar and the Babylonians. Afterwards, the Philistines disappear from the written records of history.

Tyre

The next "arrow" of Amos's prophecies aimed north to the coastal city of Tyre. The city actually was on a small coastal island. The waters surrounding it gave a natural defense and provided productive harbors.

Their Sin:

Because she sold whole communities of captives to Edom, disregarding a treaty of brotherhood, Amos 1:9b NIV

Like the Philistines in the previous verses, Tyre sold Jewish captives to the Edomites as slaves. Adding to their sin was Tyre's betrayal of an agreement between them and the Hebrews.

Their Judgment:

I will send fire on the walls of Tyre that will consume her fortresses. Amos 1:10 NIV

Ultimately, Tyre fell to the forces of Alexander the Great in 322 BC. The Greeks built a causeway over 700 meters long to gain access to the city.

Edom

These judgments moved southeast of Israel to the nation of Edom. Amos already referred to Edom as recipients of the Hebrew slaves sold by the people of Tyre and Phoenicia. Remember, the Edomites were long-time cousins of the Hebrews through their common ancestors Isaac and Rebecca. They also shared a long, hostile past with the Hebrews.

Their Sin:

Because he pursued his brother with a sword
 and slaughtered the women of the land,
because his anger raged continually
 and his fury flamed unchecked, Amos 1:11b NIV

Amos condemned the Edomites for their persistent hatred of the Jews. Rather than helping their brothers, they cast off all pity. The mention of violence against women testified to the affront of their brutality.

Their Judgment:

I will send fire on Teman that will consume the fortresses of Bozrah. Amos 1:12 NIV

Temen and *Bozrah* were strong cities which no longer exist. Rather than standing impregnable, they fell severely. Edom fell to the Babylonians and later was destroyed by the Hebrew leader Judas Maccabees:

Hereupon Judas and his host turned suddenly by the way of the wilderness unto Bosora; and when he had won the city, he slew all the males with the edge of the sword, and took all their spoils, and burned the city with fire. (1 Maccabees 5:28).

Ammon

The Ammonites were descendants of Lot through the incest activities of his daughters (Genesis 19).

Their Sin:

Because he ripped open the pregnant women of Gilead in order to extend his borders, Amos 1:13b NIV

We previously read of Edom's slaughter of women. Ammon's atrocities were greater, including the brutal massacre of pregnant women. Such barbarism is a reminder of this truth: While warfare may be a "necessary evil," it is indeed evil.

Their Judgment:

> *I will set fire to the walls of Rabbah that will consume her fortresses*
> *amid war cries on the day of battle, amid violent winds on a stormy day.*
> *15 Her king will go into exile,*
> *he and his officials together, "says the Lord.* Amos 1:14-15 NIV

A possible translation of verse 15 is *Molek will go into exile*. This could be a reference to *Molech*, the chief god of Edom. Ultimately, the false god of the Ammonites could not save them.

Moab

Ruth was a Moabite who became part of Jesus' ancestry. Historically, however, the Hebrew's history with these people was antagonistic.

- In coming out of the wilderness, the Moabites refused to give the Jews passage on the major highway. Joshua 11:17
- The Moabite king hired Balaam to curse the Hebrews. Numbers 22
- The Hebrews were subject to the Moabites for 18 years. Judges 3:12-30

Their Sin:

> *Because he burned to ashes the bones of Edom's king,* Amos 2:1b

A Long Walk with the Minor Prophets

There are some things universally considered sacred and respected. Among these are burial sites and human remains. The high regard for a deceased body especially was true in the ancient Middle East. While we do not know the identity of this king of Edom referenced here, his human remains were humiliated.

This episode reminds me of a chapter in church history regarding the remains of John Wycliffe. Wycliffe was a reformer of the Christian faith who died in 1384. Frankly, he was fortunate to die a natural death and not be burned as a heretic in his lifetime. Thirty-one years after he died, Wycliffe was condemned as a heretic at the ecclesiastical Council of Constance. Thirteen years later, in the spring of 1428 (44 years after his death), Wycliffe's bones were dug up and burned at the instruction of Pope Martin V. Today we consider Wycliffe a hero of the faith.

Their Judgment:

Moab will go down in great tumult amid war cries and the blast of the trumpet.
3 I will destroy her ruler and kill all her officials with him,"says the Lord. Amos 2:2-3 NIV

In the late 8th century BC, Moab was overpowered by the Assyrians. The land eventually became the home of numerous nomadic tribes.

JUDGMENT UPON THE HEBREWS THEMSELVES

Amos' audiences certainly applauded the previous denunciations of their pagan neighbors. They wanted to hear more! Indeed, Amos had two more "arrows" of judgment to launch. Having condemned all the surrounding nations, the prophet turned his aim upon the Hebrews themselves.

The Gentile nations sinned against conscience and the laws of brotherhood and humanity. In contrast, Judah and Israel despised and rejected the very laws of God. In short, they knew God's ways better than their pagan neighbors. This only adds to the severity of their wrongs.

Judah

Their Sin

Because they have rejected the law of the Lord and have not kept his decrees,
because they have been led astray by false gods, the gods their ancestors followed, Amos 2:4b NIV

Even with the law of the Lord available to them, the nation yielded to idolatry.

Their Judgment

I will send fire on Judah that will consume the fortresses of Jerusalem. Amos 2:5 NIV

Jerusalem fell to the Babylonian forces in 584 BC. But unlike the six Gentile nations Amos denounced, the people of Judah were not destroyed. Only their buildings were devastated. While the Hebrews of Judah did go to Babylon in exile, as a people, they were spared and returned to their homeland.

Israel

This was the home of Amos' audience. They were enjoying the good life. As a result, they were confident God was pleased with them. But beneath the surface, Amos revealed multiple layers of trouble.

Their Sins:

- **Injustice**

    They sell the innocent for silver, and the needy for a pair of sandals.
    7 They trample on the heads of the poor as on the dust of the ground
    and deny justice to the oppressed. Amos 2:6b – 7 NIV

    The poor and disadvantaged were not treated with compassion. Rather they were oppressed and denied justice.

    Amos spoke a lot about their failure to care for the poor:

    Hear this word, you cows of Bashan on Mount Samaria,
    you women who oppress the poor and crush the needy Amos 4:1a NIV

    You levy a straw tax on the poor
    and impose a tax on their grain. Amos 5:11 NIV

buying the poor with silver and the needy for a pair of sandals,
selling even the sweepings with the wheat. Amos 8:6 NIV

- **Immorality**

Father and son use the same girl and so profane my holy name. Amos 2:7b NIV

The disregard of God's design for sexuality within marriage deteriorated to the point where a father and son share a common prostitute. Such prostitutes may have been part of the heathen idolatrous worship practices. Therefore, idolatry merges with their immorality.

- **Open Idolatry**

They lie down beside every altar on garments taken in pledge.
In the house of their god they drink wine taken as fines. Amos 2:8 NIV

Notice the setting for this verse: *In the house of **their god.*** Wealthy people took their debtors' garments as pledges but did not return them at sundown as the law commanded:

26 If you take your neighbor's cloak as a pledge, return it by sunset, 27 because that cloak is the only covering your neighbor has. What else can they sleep in? When they cry out to me, I will hear, for I am compassionate. Exodus 22:26-27 NIV

Amos' words pictured a sad reality: rich sinners wrapped in coats taken as collateral, visited pagan altars where they got drunk on wine purchased with the fines extracted from the poor.

Their Glorious Past

After describing their sinful present, Amos reminded them of their glorious past:

- **God led them out of Egypt**

    I brought you up out of Egypt and led you forty years in the wilderness
    to give you the land of the Amorites. Amos 2:10

- **God gave them prophets**

    "I also raised up prophets from among your children and Nazirites from among your youths. Amos 2:11a NIV

Instead of being humbled by His blessings, they rebelled. They wanted neither the message of God nor examples of Godly living.

Their Terrible Future.

"Now then, I will crush you as a cart crushes when loaded with grain.
14 The swift will not escape, the strong will not muster their strength,
    and the warrior will not save his life.

A Long Walk with the Minor Prophets

15 The archer will not stand his ground, the fleet-footed soldier will not get away,
   and the horseman will not save his life.
16 Even the bravest warriors will flee naked on that day," declares the Lord. Amos 2:13-16 NIV

In short, judgment was coming. No matter your advantages, defeat was ahead.

- The swift won't be able to escape.
- The strong won't be able to defend themselves.
- The armed will be as if unarmed.
- The horsemen will be unable to flee.
- The bravest soldiers will run away.

In 722 BC, Assyria invaded and the people of the northern nation of Israel ceased to exist.

In closing, we return to the truth featured at the beginning of this study: Yes, God blesses the righteous. But enjoying a measure of peace and prosperity does not necessarily mean God is pleased with your life. God is full of compassion. Still, He is a God who expects adherence and (in His own time and way) enforces justice. The author of Hebrews affirms this distinction:

30 For we know him who said, "It is mine to avenge; I will repay," and again, "The Lord will judge his people." 31 It is a dreadful thing to fall into the hands of the living God. Hebrews 10:30-31 NIV

A Long Walk with the Minor Prophets

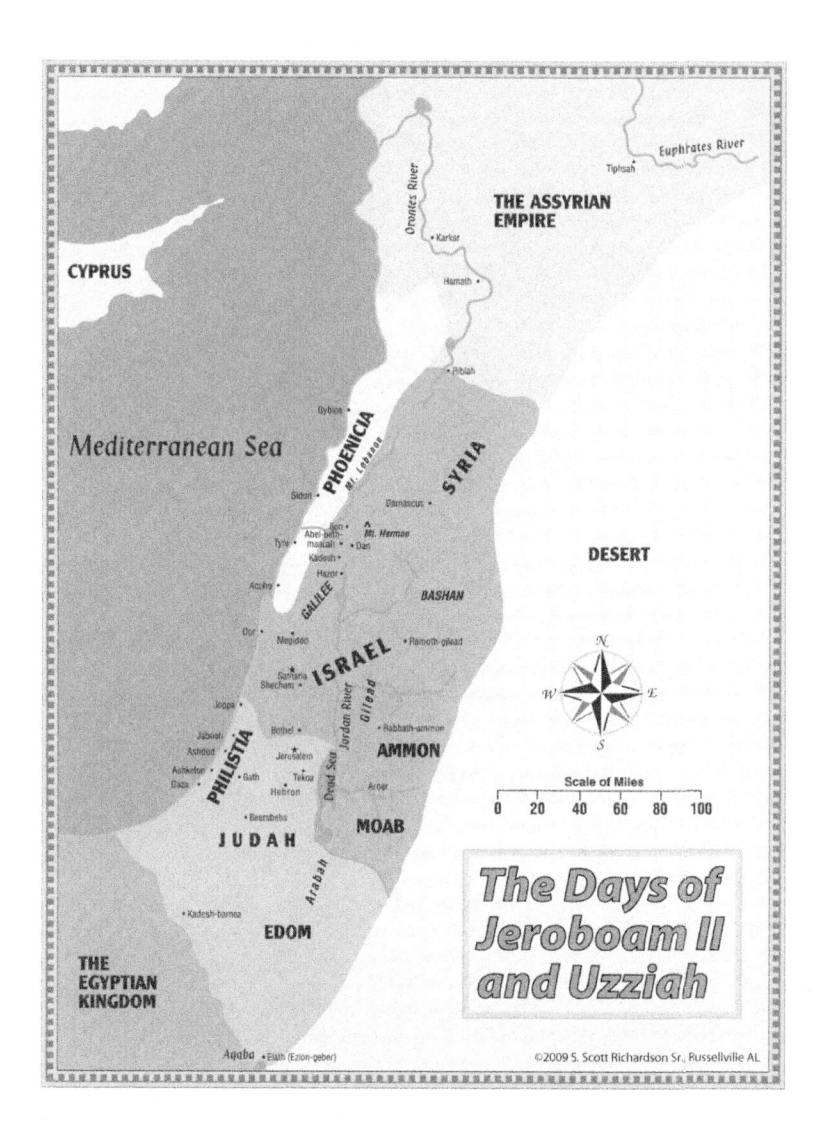

A Long Walk with the Minor Prophets

6 – AMOS
Chapters 3 - 5
Hear This Word

In chapters 1 and 2 Amos spoke to nations all around Israel before finally giving a word to this northern kingdom of the Hebrews. His prophecies followed an ever-tightening geographic circle before hitting their primary target: Israel. It was as if he was saying, *Now that I have your attention, here is what God told me to say to YOU!* Each of the next three chapters begin with the same opening:

Hear this word…

The admonishment was first to listen. Effective hearing is essential to the receiving of any message. What prevents you from hearing?

Not listening

> We simply can ignore what is being said, even from the Lord. The author of Hebrews warned: *Today, if you hear His voice, do not harden your hearts.* Hebrews 3:15

Selective hearing

> We easily can dismiss a message because it is not what we want to hear. Paul cautioned Timothy regarding this tendency:

> *For the time will come when people will not put up with sound doctrine. Instead, to suit their own desires, they will gather around them a great number of teachers to say what their itching ears want to hear.* 2 Timothy 4:3 NIV

With the repeated command to *Hear this word,* Amos called for their full attention as he pointed their awareness to a key theme in each chapter.

IDENTIFICATION – Chapter 3

Having gathered his audience's attention, Amos took time to explain some things about their identity.

You Are Chosen

Hear this word, people of Israel, the word the Lord has spoken against you—against the whole family I brought up out of Egypt: "You only have I chosen of all the families of the earth; Amos 3:1-2a NIV

It is nice to be chosen. Some are chosen for a job. Some are chosen for a team. I am still amazed that my wife chose me as her spouse! Amos reminded the Israelites of their status as God's uniquely chosen people. It was an honored distinction carried by both the Hebrews of the Old Testament and the disciples of the New Testament.

The Lord your God has chosen you out of all the peoples on the face of the earth to be his people, his treasured possession. Deuteronomy 7:6 NIV

You did not choose me, but I chose you and appointed you so that you might go and bear fruit John 15:16 NIV

You Are Responsible

therefore I will punish you for all your sins." Amos 3:2b NIV

Being chosen did not exempt them from responsibility. Neither did being chosen grant them an excuse for their sins. Instead, being chosen rightfully motivates people toward holy living. They (and we) were responsible to love God and obey Him. When they did not, God was responsible to chasten them in love, seeking to bring them back to Himself.

You Are Informed

Verses 3-8 covered a list of causes and effects.

> *Do two walk together unless they have agreed to do so?* Amos 3:3 NIV

> *Does a bird swoop down to a trap on the ground when no bait is there?* Amos 3:5a NIV

> *When a trumpet sounds in a city, do not the people tremble?* Amos 3:6 NIV

There is a pattern and a process for these examples. And there is a pattern God follows regarding his plans:

> *Surely the Sovereign Lord does nothing without revealing his plan to his servants the prophets.* Amos 3:7 NIV

It is a bit like saying, *You were told. You are without excuse. You can't say you were not warned.* One of our church's deacons works as a referee for high school football games. He reports that in certain situations he gives players a warning before he actually throws a penalty flag. They cannot say they were not warned.

You Are Headed for Trouble

Frankly, at this time, such a dire forecast appeared unlikely. When Amos prophesied, things looked good. Prosperity was growing and peace was prevailing. But Amos informed Israel they were on a slippery downward slope.

> *Therefore this is what the Sovereign Lord says:*
> *"An enemy will overrun your land,*
>   *pull down your strongholds and plunder your fortresses."*
> Amos 3:11 NIV

The title *Sovereign Lord* often is translated *Lord God*. In Hebrew, two names for God are placed side by side: *ădōnāy* and *yawah*. We sometimes state multiple titles together to emphasize stature and authority. Thus, a minister may be referred to as *Right Reverend*. A king can be called his *Royal Highness*.

God spoke from His sovereign authority. The enemy heading to overrun the land was Assyria. While Israel looked sound, in less than 50 years (722 BC) it fell to the Assyrian empire.

Like Israel of old, nations, entities, and people measure themselves by their wealth. Our answer to many problems is to throw money at it. While money can grant a level of security, it is not the source of ultimate security. There are real problems no amount of money in the world can solve.

ACCUSATION – Chapter 4

Like an indictment, in this message Amos pointed out some particular sins against Israel.

Extravagance

Hear this word, you cows of Bashan on Mount Samaria,
 you women who oppress the poor and crush the needy
  and say to your husbands, "Bring us some drinks!" Amos 4:1 NIV

The command to *Hear this word* was addressed to the society women. These ladies lived in great luxury and entitlement while the poor struggled. (For the record, I do not recommend ever referring to women as "cows.")

The Sovereign Lord has sworn by his holiness:
 "The time will surely come when you will be taken away with hooks,
  the last of you with fishhooks. Amos 4:2 NIV

The people who lived in luxury would be led away like animals, either into captivity or to death. Because they oppressed the poor, they had things money could buy. But they did not have the things money could not buy.

It is no sin to have means. It can be a sign of responsible decision making. But there remains the question: *What do you do with it?* Paul gave Timothy this commission.

Command those who are rich in this present world not to be arrogant nor to put their hope in wealth, which is so uncertain, but to put their hope in God, who richly provides us with everything for our enjoyment. 1 Timothy 6:17 NIV

Hypocrisy

> *"Go to Bethel and sin; go to Gilgal and sin yet more.*
> *Bring your sacrifices every morning, your tithes every three years.*
> *5 Burn leavened bread as a thank offering and brag about your freewill offerings—*
> *boast about them, you Israelites, for this is what you love to do,"*
> *declares the Sovereign Lord.* Amos 4:4-5 NIV

They went to the holy places. They gave their sacrifices. They contributed their tithes. But their gifts did not impress the Lord. He saw what was in their hearts. They bragged about their offerings. But it was not the Lord who received glory. Jesus also cautioned about performing righteous acts for our own praise.

> *So when you give to the needy, do not announce it with trumpets, as the hypocrites do in the synagogues and on the streets, to be honored by others. Truly I tell you, they have received their reward in full.* Matthew 6:2 NIV

It is incumbent upon God's people to examine their hearts and make certain their motives are right. What they do must glorify the Lord and not themselves. Even so, there is a hypocrite in every pew of our churches. We all fall short of this noble ideal. Unfortunately, not all people admit to this.

Stubbornness

Amos reminded Israel that God had tried to discipline His people. Unfortunately, they did not submit to His will. Rather, they stubbornly continued in their corruption. Notice that after each effort to exert discipline, the Lord laments <u>yet you have not returned to me.</u>

- **Famine**

    "I gave you empty stomachs in every city and lack of bread in every town,
    yet you have not returned to me," declares the Lord.
    Amos 4:6 NIV

- **Drought**

    "I also withheld rain from you when the harvest was still three months away.
    yet you have not returned to me," declares the Lord.
    Amos 4:7a, 8b NIV

- **Destruction of Crops**

    "Many times I struck your gardens and vineyards,
         destroying them with blight and mildew.
    Locusts devoured your fig and olive trees,
         yet you have not returned to me," declares the Lord.
    Amos 4:9 NIV

Centuries before, Moses warned their ancestors that God's curses would follow disobedience:

38 You will sow much seed in the field but you will harvest little, because locusts will devour it. 39 You will plant vineyards and cultivate them but you will not drink the wine or gather the grapes, because worms will eat them.
Deuteronomy 28:38-39 NIV

- **Sickness**

    "I sent plagues among you as I did to Egypt.

> *yet you have not returned to me,"* declares the Lord. Amos 4:10 NIV

Shortly after the plagues on Egypt, God promised immunity from the plagues of Egypt if they attended to God's ways.

> *26 He said, "If you listen carefully to the Lord your God and do what is right in his eyes, if you pay attention to his commands and keep all his decrees, I will not bring on you any of the diseases I brought on the Egyptians, for I am the Lord, who heals you."* Exodus 15:26 NIV

- **Defeat**

> *"I overthrew some of you as I overthrew Sodom and Gomorrah.*
> *You were like a burning stick snatched from the fire,*
> *yet you have not returned to me,"* declares the Lord. Amos 4:11 NIV

Unfortunately, God's people allowed each opportunity to recognize the Lord's discipline to slip away. None of these occasions brought them to repentance. Instead, this was the result:

> *"Therefore this is what I will do to you, Israel, and because I will do this to you, Israel,*
> *prepare to meet your God." Amos* 4:12 NIV

For a humble believer, meeting God is the greatest end. For one who dismisses the Lord's hand, meeting God is a dreadful end. Fear of judgment may not be the highest motive for obeying God, but the Lord will accept it.

Amos provided us with an incredible phrase with which to live our lives. Each day, *prepare to meet your God* and not just in death. Prepare to face the reality of the God who is so easily dismissed by others.

LAMENTATION – Chapter 5

Hear this word, Israel, this lament I take up concerning you:
"Fallen is Virgin Israel, never to rise again,
deserted in her own land, with no one to lift her up." Amos 5:1-2 NIV

A lament is known as words of grief, regret, sorrow, and pain. I have conducted over 500 memorial services in my four decades as a pastor. Some funerals are celebrations of a life well lived, filled with devotion to faith and family. On the other hand, some funerals are *Laments*. These are times of great sorrow and loss.

Amos called Israel a *Virgin*. It is a word identifying a woman of young age. The saddest funerals are those held for the death of a young person. The grief of a parent burying a child is the heaviest I know.

In this chapter, the Lord gives Israel two worthwhile pursuits.

Seek the Lord and Live

4 This is what the Lord says to Israel:"Seek me and live;
5 do not seek Bethel, do not go to Gilgal, do not journey to Beersheba.
For Gilgal will surely go into exile, and Bethel will be reduced to nothing."
6 Seek the Lord and live, Amos 5:4-6a NIV

For what are you looking? For what are you living? Your answers to these questions determine the Master over your life. Jesus states a fitting and higher search:

> *Seek ye first the Kingdom of God and His righteousness. And all these things will be added unto you.* Matthew 6:33

The people sought out holy places like Bethel and Gilgal to aid their condition. But a change in geography did not overcome a flaw in character. Ralph Waldo Emerson put it this way: *No change of circumstances can repair a defect of character.*

Seek the Good and Live

Verses 7-13 speak of their sins of injustice, corrupt courts, oppressing the poor and taking bribes. As an alternative, Amos offered this alternative direction:

Seek good, not evil, that you may live.
Then the Lord God Almighty will be with you, just as you say he is.
Hate evil, love good; maintain justice in the courts. Amos 5:14-15a NIV

Remember, Amos prophesied to a tremendously prosperous land. The economy was booming. The citizens were convinced God was showing favor on them. But they were wrong. If they wished for God to be with them, they should seek after the Lord's character and desires.

Still, there was hope. In the midst of such a bleak forecast, Amos offered this possibility:

Perhaps the Lord God Almighty will have mercy on the remnant of Joseph. Amos 5:14-15 NIV

It reminds me of Nineveh's response after Jonah prophesied of their pending destruction:

Who knows? God may yet relent and with compassion turn from his fierce anger so that we will not perish." Jonah 3:9 NIV

Could it be the same for Israel? Disaster was coming. But who knew what God would do if people turned to Him? Remember, ten righteous people could have spared Sodom and Gomorrah. In Nineveh's case, all the people repented. But in Israel, there was no repentance.

In Charles Dicken's *A Christmas Carol* Ebenezer Scrooge is visited on Christmas Eve by three ghosts. During their visits, he saw his own wickedness for what it was. He saw the love and kindness of those people he mistreated for his own gain. And he saw his own death. After these experiences, he woke up on Christmas morning a changed man. He had seen the bleak future of his wicked life and changed his ways. He had listened. A similar outcome was possible for Israel if they had sought God and sought goodness.

In the armed services, upon receiving instructions, the servicemen and women may respond by saying " HUA!" The acronym stands for **H**eard, **U**nderstood, and **A**cknowledged. This is the reaction God desired from His people in response to the words of the prophet.

Hear the Word – Identification of who you are.

Understand your mistakes as the sins for which you are accused.
Acknowledge – Respond by seeking God and His goodness.

7 – AMOS
Chapters 7 - 9
Lord God Almighty

Our previous lesson recognized how Amos affirmed the authority of the Lord by pairing two divine titles: "Sovereign Lord" (or "Lord God" in some translations). Amos also utilized an even stronger series of divine titles: *The Lord God Almighty*. Of the twenty-seven times this designation appears in the Old Testament, seven of these occurrences are within the nine chapters of the little book of Amos.

The Hebrew reading is 'ăḏōnāy yᵊhōvâ 'ĕlōhîm ṣāḇā'

Adonay = Used as a proper name for God
Yahweh = The sacred name for God
Elohim = A general word for God.
Saba = A mass number… of military (physical army) or angels (spiritual army)

Most English versions translate this phrase: *The Lord God of hosts*. Again, it is a respectful recognition of God's great authority. The affirmation is fitting. At the core of Israel's sin was their disrespect and dismissal of the Lord and His ways.

In this study we will survey the final few chapters of Amos. Six characteristics of *The Lord God Almighty* stand out. What does Amos say about *The Lord God Almighty?*

THE LORD GOD ALMIGHTY'S JUDGMENT IS CERTAIN

> *This is what the Sovereign Lord showed me: He was preparing swarms of locusts after the king's share had been harvested and just as the late crops were coming up. 2 When they had stripped the land*

clean, I cried out, "Sovereign Lord, forgive! How can Jacob survive? He is so small!" 3 So the Lord relented. Amos 7:1-3a NIV

In our study of Joel we saw the devastation of a locust plague. Here, in response to Amos' appeal, the Lord relented from sending this outbreak. But in the next verse, God shows Amos another expression of judgment:

4 This is what the Sovereign Lord showed me: The Sovereign Lord was calling for judgment by fire; it dried up the great deep and devoured the land. 5 Then I cried out, "Sovereign Lord, I beg you, stop! How can Jacob survive? He is so small!" 6 So the Lord relented.

Again, Amos begged for this tragedy to not occur. And again, the Lord relented. You may conclude God's judgment to be *less than certain*. However, the Lord's next words were definitive.

Then the Lord said, "Look, I am setting a plumb line among my people Israel; I will spare them no longer.
  "The high places of Isaac will be destroyed
    and the sanctuaries of Israel will be ruined;
      with my sword I will rise against the house of Jeroboam."
Amos 7:8b-9 NIV

It is an ominous word. The nation had gone too far. And this time Amos offered no appeal for leniency.

The word translated "plumb line" ("anak") occurs only in this passage in the Hebrew Bible. Builders utilize plumb lines to ensure that walls and structures are built vertically. If a wall continues to be built "out of plumb" it eventually will fall. Israel's lack of justice for the poor and their misuse of religion was "out of plumb" with God's expectations. Their neglect eventually toppled them. Frankly, their demise did not require God's hand to interject a locust plague or a fire. Israel's own sin caused their collapse.

THE LORD GOD ALMIGHTY'S MESSAGE IS UNDENIABLE

The second half of chapter 7 follows a conversation between Amos and Amaziah. *Then Amaziah said to Amos, "Get out, you seer! Go back to the land of Judah. Earn your bread there and do your prophesying there.* Amos 7:12 NIV

Amaziah was Israel's lead priest appointed by King Jeroboam II. He called Amos a "seer," meaning someone with insights. But in this case the word was spoken in a derogatory manner. While Amos prophesied against Israel, he actually was from the southern nation of Judah. Naturally, Amaziah did not like hearing God's instruction from a non-member of their community. Most people do not want to hear critical judgments, especially from an outsider.

Amos did not like the assignment either. Why would he do this? Why would he face an audience bound to be hostile to him? The simple answer is because God gave him the message.

14 Amos answered Amaziah, "I was neither a prophet nor the son of a prophet, but I was a shepherd, and I also took care of sycamore-fig trees. 15 But the Lord took me from tending the flock and said to me, 'Go, prophesy to my people Israel.' 16 Now then, hear the word of the Lord Amos 7:14-16a NIV

Amos was not a prophet by birth or occupation. Still, God gave him a message. Amaziah had position, wealth, political authority, and reputation. Amos, on the other hand, had the word of the Lord. This supersedes all else. When the disciples were told not to teach in Jesus' name, they affirmed the *undeniable* nature of God's word:

Then Peter and the other apostles answered and said, We ought to obey God rather than men. Acts 5:29 NIV

THE LORD GOD ALMIGHTY'S TIMING IS RIGHT

This is what the Sovereign Lord showed me: a basket of ripe fruit. 2 "What do you see, Amos?" he asked. "A basket of ripe fruit," I answered. Then the Lord said to me, "The time is ripe for my people Israel; I will spare them no longer. Amos 8:1-2 NIV

Just as a specific time arrives when fruit ripens, there also comes a time when God's patience runs out. Amos described the misdeeds bringing them to this fruition. These words particularly identified Israel's faults through deceptive selling.

skimping on the measure, boosting the price
   and cheating with dishonest scales,
6 buying the poor with silver
   and the needy for a pair of sandals,
   selling even the sweepings with the wheat. Amos 8:5-6 NIV

The law demanded they use accurate weights and measures. But the sellers cared only for their own profitability. Toward this end they utilized outlandish prices, dishonest weights, and swept chaff off the floor to mix in as "filler" within the useful grain.

By contrast, God's judgment was like a great reversal of the status quo:

> The practice of nature will be reversed:

> *I will make the sun go down at noon* Amos 8:9b NIV

The intent of religious festivals is reversed:

> *I will turn your religious festivals into mourning*
> *and all your singing into weeping.* Amos 8:10a NIV

The nature of hunger and thirst is reversed:

> *"The days are coming," declares the Sovereign Lord,*
> *"when I will send a famine through the land—*
> *not a famine of food or a thirst for water,*
> *but a famine of hearing the words of the Lord.* Amos 8:11 NIV

Theirs was not a famine of food but a famine of spiritual nourishment. We hunger and thirst for what is absent. Israel had plenty of "religion" but no word from the Lord.

The strong reverse and become weak:

> *In that day the lovely young women and strong young men will faint because of thirst. Amos* 8:13 NIV

When even the young faint, things are bad.

Earlier in the book, Amos voices God's scorn for their religious practices.

> *"I hate, I despise your religious festivals;*
> *your assemblies are a stench to me.* Amos 5:21 NIV

Take a moment to complete this sentence: *God is not interested in our worship if….*

Possible answers include:
...*our worship does not change our behavior.*
...*our worship is only for show.*
...*our worship is insincere.*
...*our worship is only going through religious motions.*

Israel appeared economically and militarily healthy. But genuine <u>health</u> for communities, churches, families, and individuals is far more dependent upon spiritual health. Spiritual health protects the weak. It does not trample upon them.

THE LORD GOD ALMIGHTY'S JUDGMENT IS INESCAPEABLE

Chapter 9 opens with the announcement that there is no retreat from God's judgment.

Not one will get away,
  none will escape.
2 Though they dig down to the depths below,
  from there my hand will take them.
Though they climb up to the heavens above,
  from there I will bring them down.
3 Though they hide themselves on the top of Carmel,
  there I will hunt them down and seize them. Amos 9:1-3 NIV

Amos' declaration sounded like a classic, *You can run but you cannot hide* scenario...because it is! No route granted escape from the imposing judgment of the Lord.

A story from the Civil War era tells of a young soldier brought before General Robert E. Lee. The young man was charged with some offense and was so afraid that he shook. Wanting to be reassuring General Lee looked at him and said, "Don't be afraid son, you'll get justice here." The young soldier replied, "That's why I'm shaking, sir."

THE LORD GOD ALMIGHTY'S JUDGMENT IS GREAT

"Lord" "God" and "Almighty" are far more than mere titles. Our Heavenly Father genuinely IS GREAT! Amos reminds them of the greatness of the God they claimed they were worshipping.

The Lord, the Lord Almighty—
he touches the earth and it melts,
    and all who live in it mourn;
the whole land rises like the Nile,
    then sinks like the river of Egypt;
6 he builds his lofty palace in the heavens
    and sets its foundation on the earth;
he calls for the waters of the sea
    and pours them out over the face of the land—
    the Lord is his name. Amos 9:5-6 NIV

Israel was guilty of a dismissive attitude toward God. They disregarded the awesome greatness of God through their self-serving practices. Even today, many people choose to live however they wish while granting the Lord mere "token" attention at best.

THE LORD GOD ALMIGHTY'S FINAL WORD IS HOPE

Despite numerous words of condemnation and judgment, Amos closed on a note of hope.

"In that day

"I will restore David's fallen shelter—
I will repair its broken walls
and restore its ruins—
and will rebuild it as it used to be, Amos 9:11 NIV

Like a rickety shack, David's dynasty was about to collapse. But one day God would restore and rebuild and establish the kingdom He promised. I love that God is in the *restoration business.*

Years ago, a church member named Gary Robbins lived near our campus. In his retirement, Gary restored old furniture. I routinely saw him working in his driveway on a china cabinet, a dresser, or a buffet. He would take these ugly and worn pieces of furniture and restore their beauty and usefulness. When Gary passed away, I used "restoration" as the theme for his funeral. I noted how God takes our weathered brokenness, restoring us to His beautiful design. In eternity, we will experience the Lord's ultimate restoration.

Amos continues with a declaration of the future fruitfulness of the land:

13 "The days are coming," declares the Lord,
"when the reaper will be overtaken by the plowman
and the planter by the one treading grapes.
New wine will drip from the mountains
and flow from all the hills,
14   and I will bring my people Israel back from exile. Amos 9:13-14 NIV

After so many prophecies about decline, what a wonderful picture of blessed abundance and productivity! Amos' final word declared this assurance:

A Long Walk with the Minor Prophets

15 I will plant Israel in their own land,
   never again to be uprooted
   from the land I have given them,"
says the Lord your God. Amos 9:15 NIV

Do not miss this final divine title Amos uses: *the Lord* YOUR GOD! What an encouragement! In so many ways, Amos' audience gave up on the Lord. But God did not give up on them! Despite their rebellion, He was still their God and still granted His covenant promises.

JUDGMENT FIRE by Jay McCluskey

Sung to the tune of *Ring of Fire* by Johnny Cash, June Carter Cash, and Merle Kilgore.

I will send a fire… Amos 1:4, 7, 10, 12, 2:2, 2:5.

Edom and the Moabites
Syria, Gaza, Ammonites
Israel, Judah, and Tyre
They'll all fall into a judgment fire

God will send His sovereign judgment fire.
You'll go down, down, down,
Your days will get quite dire.
You should turn, turn, turn,
And live much higher.
And live much higher.

God will send His sovereign judgment fire.
You'll go down, down, down,
Your days will get quite dire.
You should turn, turn, turn,
And live much higher.
And live much higher.

Israel, you were so blessed.
Now Amos says your world's a mess.
Hypocrisy, and cheating the weak.
Things look good now, 'till God turns on the heat.

God will send His sovereign judgment fire.
You'll go down, down, down,
Your days will get quite dire.
You should turn, turn, turn,
And live much higher. And live much higher. (Repeat)

A Long Walk with the Minor Prophets

8 – HOSEA
Chapters 1 - 3
Preaching Without Words

You cannot say they were not warned.

Despite warnings from the prophet Amos, the Northern Kingdom of Israel continued in their idolatry and immorality. As shared in our previous lessons, the prosperity of their time made these Hebrews less inclined to repent and change.

INTRODUCTION

Along came a prophet from Israel to Israel: Hosea. Hosea is considered a "minor prophet" despite having 14 chapters in his writings. For the record, Zechariah matches Hosea as the longest of the Minor Prophets also with 14 chapters. Ironically, Daniel is considered a "major prophet" with 12 chapters.

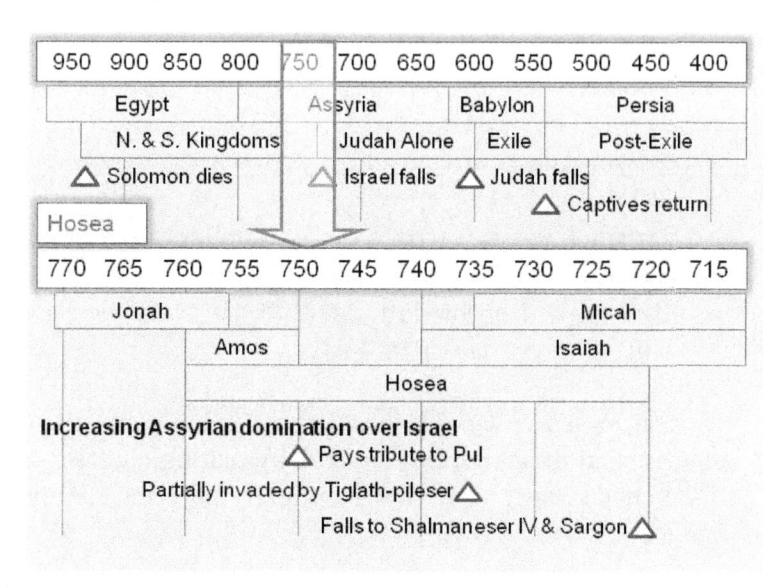

950	900	850	800	750	700	650	600	550	500	450	400
	Egypt				Assyria		Babylon		Persia		
		N. & S. Kingdoms			Judah Alone	Exile		Post-Exile		
	△ Solomon dies		△ Israel falls	△ Judah falls				
						△ Captives return		

Hosea

770	765	760	755	750	745	740	735	730	725	720	715
Jonah								Micah			
		Amos						Isaiah			
				Hosea							

Increasing Assyrian domination over Israel
△ Pays tribute to Pul
Partially invaded by Tiglath-pileser △
Falls to Shalmaneser IV & Sargon △

101

As a contemporary of Jonah, Amos, Isaiah, and Micah, Hosea tried to deliver God's message over about a 40-year span: roughly 760 BC to 720 BC. So many prophets ministering in such a tight window of time is impressive.

Only 15 years later, around 735 BC, the Assyrians partially invaded the land under Tiglath-Pileser (2 Kings 15:29). Finally, around 720 BC the Northern Kingdom fell to the Assyrians. Again, you cannot say the people were not warned.

The Method

The title for this study, *Preaching Without Words*, comes from a famous quote attributed to Francis of Assisi:

- *Preach the gospel at all times and if necessary, use words.*

On numerous occasions God called prophets to communicate a message through their actions rather than their voice:

- Isaiah walked around like a prisoner of war (Isaiah 20).
- Jeremiah carried a yoke on his shoulders (Jeremiah 27:1-2).
- Ezekiel laid on his left side 390 days and his right side 40 days (Ezekiel 4:4-6).

Hosea *preached without words* through his marriage to Gomer and the children produced by that union. This is the better-known portion of Hosea's prophecies and the subject of today's lesson.

DEMONSTRATION – Chapter 1:1-3

The book opens with an unusual "action sermon" God called Hosea to take:

2 When the Lord began to speak through Hosea, the Lord said to him, "Go, marry a promiscuous woman and have children with her, for like an adulterous wife this land is guilty of unfaithfulness to the Lord." 3 So he married Gomer daughter of Diblaim Hosea 1:2-3a NIV

Surprisingly, God commissioned His prophet to enter an *unequally yoked* marriage relationship. God orchestrated a plan to use Gomer's waywardness to illustrate His love. Remember one of the heroes of Hebrew history is Rahab, who was a prostitute. Gomer's story of unfaithfulness reaffirms the lesson that God's kingdom can use anybody.

In scripture, the marriage covenant is often compared to a covenant relationship between God and His people. Both covenants expect 100% faithfulness. And both require grace to endure. Here, the link between Hosea and Gomer demonstrated the bond between the Lord and Israel.

DESCRIPTION - Chapter 1:3-10

Three children enter the union. God gave each of these significant names.

...she conceived and bore him a son. 4 Then the Lord said to Hosea, "Call him Jezreel, because I will soon punish the house of Jehu for the massacre at Jezreel, and I will put an end to the kingdom of Israel. 5 In that day I

will break Israel's bow in the Valley of Jezreel." Hosea 1:3b-5 NIV

The name *Jezreel* means *God scatters.* It is a reference to a harsh and cruel incident carried out in Jezreel where Jehu cruelly executed the family of Ahab (2 Kings 9-10). Thus, the name of Hosea and Gomer's firstborn indicated God would retaliate for the shedding of innocent blood and put an end to Jehu's dynasty. This avengement took place in 752 BC.

6 Gomer conceived again and gave birth to a daughter. Then the Lord said to Hosea, "Call her Lo-Ruhamah (which means "not loved"), for I will no longer show love to Israel, that I should at all forgive them. 7 Yet I will show love to Judah; and I will save them—not by bow, sword or battle, or by horses and horsemen, but I, the Lord their God, will save them." Hosea 1:6-7 NIV

This daughter is named, *Lo-Ruhamah*. Her name means, *Not loved* or *Not Pitied*. The expression also carried the idea of *Not Protected*. The name declared God would withhold His blessing and allow the Assyrians to take Israel.

8 After she had weaned Lo-Ruhamah, Gomer had another son. 9 Then the Lord said, "Call him Lo-Ammi (which means "not my people"), for you are not my people, and I am not your God. Hosea 1:3b-8 NIV

God said to name this third child *Lo-Ammi*. This name means *Not my people* or *Not my child*. What an exceptional name!

Here is a word of advice for expectant parents pondering what to name their forthcoming baby: Stand on your porch and shout the name as loudly as you can. That is the way the name often will be heard! Imagine Hosea calling his youngest son and essentially saying, *Not Mine! Not Mine!*

I lightheartedly say that some parents curse their children by the name they give them.

- If, like me, your parents call you by a nickname, you are cursed to explain your legal name the rest of your life.
- If your parents call you by your middle name, you are cursed to correct people who call you by your legal first name.
- If your parents spell your name in an unusual way, you are cursed to always offer the proper way to spell your name.

Of course, these are "mild curses." The names of Hosea's children indicated the severe damage to the covenant between Israel and the Lord. Their rebellion cost them God's loving protection and family bond.

In the transition into chapter two, the narrative quickly reveals these children one day will receive new, more favorable names.

In the place where it was said to them, 'You are not my people,' they will be called 'children of the living God.' Hosea 1:10b NIV

"Say of your brothers, 'My people,' and of your sisters, 'My loved one.' Hosea 2:1

Perhaps Hosea did not want the reader to dwell on his children's dreadful names. Thus, he hastily mentioned the new favorable names in their destiny.

TRANSGRESSION - Chapter 2

This chapter is written in first person voice from God's perspective. Here the Lord pointed out the fact of Israel's transgressions and their consequences.

God said to the children of Israel:

> *"Rebuke your mother, rebuke her,*
> *for she is not my wife,*
> *and I am not her husband.* Hosea 2:2a NIV

In the following verses God spoke to His bride about what would happen if they continued in unfaithfulness. Notice all the expressions that start with the words *I will...*

> *Otherwise I will strip her naked* Hosea 2:3a NIV

> *I will make her like a desert,*
> *turn her into a parched land*, Hosea 2:3b NIV

> *I will not show my love to her children*, Hosea 2:4 NIV

> *Therefore I will block her path with thornbushes;*
> *I will wall her in so that she cannot find her way.* Hosea 2:6 NIV

> *"Therefore I will take away my grain when it ripens,*
> *and my new wine when it is ready.*

> *I will take back my wool and my linen,* Hosea 2:9a NIV
>
> *I will stop all her celebrations:*
> *her yearly festivals, her New Moons,* Hosea 2:11a NIV
>
> *I will punish her for the days*
> *she burned incense to the Baals;* Hosea 2:13a NIV

Immediately following this list of transgressions and resulting hardships, God's treatment of Israel takes a great reversal. He approaches His bride in a gesture of grand courtship and restoration. Notice again God's use of the expression *I will.*

> *"Therefore I am now going to allure her;*
> *I will lead her into the wilderness*
> *and speak tenderly to her.* Hosea 2:14 NIV
>
> *There I will give her back her vineyards,* Hosea 2:15a NIV
>
> *I will remove the names of the Baals from her lips;*
> *no longer will their names be invoked.* Hosea 2:17 NIV
>
> *In that day I will make a covenant for them* Hosea 2:18a NIV
>
> *I will betroth you to me forever;*
> *I will betroth you in righteousness and justice,*
> *in love and compassion.*
> *20 I will betroth you in faithfulness,*
> *and you will acknowledge the Lord.* Hosea 2:19-20 NIV

Their new relationship would endure forever. The covenant lasts because of God's devotion to act towards them in righteousness, justice, love, compassion, and faithfulness. Also, this new covenant brings about new names for Hosea's children:

> *I will plant her for myself in the land;*
> *I will show my love to the one I called 'Not my loved one.'*
> *I will say to those called 'Not my people' 'You are my people';*
> *and they will say, 'You are my God.'"* Hosea 2:23 NIV

We saw earlier that Jezreel means *God scatters*. But *scattering* is also the method a farmer uses to sow (plant) his seed. God will *scatter/plant* Israel for Himself. The daughter and son named "not loved" and "not my child" will receive names with opposite meanings. As the Lord loves and claims them, they respond fittingly: *You are my God!*

RESTORATION - Chapter 3

We turn to a short story about Gomer's restoration. Apparently, Gomer left Hosea. Her life descended to the point where she was auctioned for sale in a local marketplace. Here God gave Hosea the responsibility to buy back his own wife.

The Lord said to me, "Go, show your love to your wife again, though she is loved by another man and is an adulteress. Love her as the Lord loves the Israelites, though they turn to other gods and love the sacred raisin cakes."

2 So I bought her for fifteen shekels of silver and about a homer and a lethek of barley. 3 Then I told her, "You are to live with me many days; you must not be a prostitute or be intimate with any man, and I will behave the same way toward you." Hosea 3:1-3 NIV

This again is preaching without words. Through his actions Hosea pictured how God responds in His relationship to Israel:

4 For the Israelites will live many days without king or prince, without sacrifice or sacred stones, without ephod or household gods.

In short, they were without everything they previously claimed to depend upon in their rebellious times. Today, we may mistakenly depend upon money, strength, influence, health, or intelligence.

5 Afterward the Israelites will return and seek the Lord their God and David their king. They will come trembling to the Lord and to his blessings in the last days. Hosea 3:4-5 NIV

After their restoration, there is respect for the Lord and His blessings. The key word is *return*. It is used 22 times in Hosea's prophecy. The intent of Hosea's preaching without words was to inspire Israel to return from their devastation. To be redeemed and restored, Israel needs to say: *Come, and let us return to the Lord.* Hosea 6:1a NIV

This is the summary of Hosea's message:

Return, Israel, to the Lord your God.

Your sins have been your downfall!
2 Take words with you and return to the Lord.
Say to him: "Forgive all our sins
and receive us graciously, that we may offer the fruit of our lips. Hosea 14:1-2 NIV

The people enjoyed the blessing of divine gifts, but failed to honor the giver. God, on the other hand, is holy and must deal with sin. He promises to forgive and to receive all who trust Him.

A Long Walk with the Minor Prophets

9 – HOSEA
Chapters 4 - 6
The Courtroom

The first three chapters of Hosea described a variety of settings:

- A wedding ceremony, *Go, marry a promiscuous woman...* Hosea 1:2b
- A maternity ward, *she conceived and bore him a son.* Hosea 1:3b
- And a slave auction, *So I bought her for fifteen shekels of silver and about a homer and a lethek of barley* Hosea 3:2

In chapters 4-6, Hosea added another venue to his prophecies against Israel: A Courtroom. In these words of prophecy, Israel is put on trial and found lacking.

CHARGES AGAINST ISRAEL

> *Hear the word of the Lord, you Israelites,*
>   *because the Lord has a charge to bring*
>   *against you who live in the land*: Hosea 4:1a NIV

Trials open with the prosecution presenting their charges against the accused. Israel was reproached for numerous wrongs. The charges brought against Israel fall into two categories.

Sins of Omission

> *"There is no faithfulness, no love,*
>   *no acknowledgment of God in the land.* Hosea 4:1b NIV

A familiar country music song summarizes the singer's relationship failure in the words *It's not what I did. It's what I didn't do.* Hosea began with a list of what Israel did **not** do. Israel did not show faithfulness to God. Israel did not show love. Israel did not acknowledge God. In short, Israel did not live differently from the pagan nations around them.

Faith is merely a label if it fails to inspire holy actions. In reality, this is no faith at all. Life devoted to the Lord must be different than the life of a pagan worshipping a false God or an atheist who does not accept the existence of God.

Sins of Commission

There is only cursing, lying and murder,
 stealing and adultery;
they break all bounds,
 and bloodshed follows bloodshed. Hosea 4:2 NIV

The disobedient actions the people practiced were the opposite of what they were omitting. They did whatever was necessary to acquire what they desired, even to the point of violence and murder.

Their charges included multiple violations of the Ten Commandments:

> Cursing – *Thou shall not use the Lord's name in vain.*
> Lying – *Thou shall not bear false witness.*
> Stealing – *Thou shalt not steal.*
> Adultery – *They shall not commit adultery.*

Some crimes are misdemeanors, breaches of less severe laws. But in their case, Israel was guilty of violating some of God's *Top Ten* laws!

PENALTIES

In court, the penalties passed down to the guilty include the loss of things like freedom, money, and reputation. Hosea informed the Israelites of the losses ahead because of their disobedience.

Loss of Nature's Fruitfulness

Because of this the land dries up,
  and all who live in it waste away;
the beasts of the field, the birds in the sky
  and the fish in the sea are swept away. Hosea 4:3 NIV

We saw similar words in chapter two where God repeats the phrase *I will*. Those words also described how the consequences of sin impacts the agricultural viability of the land.

Loss of their Priestly Status

"Because you have rejected knowledge,
  I also reject you as my priests; Hosea 4:6a NIV

While this prophecy could be against the men in Israel who served formally as priests, the tone of the passage implies the rejection of the entire priestly nation. A priest was to be a mediator between humans and the Lord. When God called Abraham, He stated His intention for all the patriarch's descendants to be a channel of blessing.

and all peoples on earth
  will be blessed through you. Genesis 12:3b NIV

The New Testament church is described with this same "priestly" assignment:

> *To him who loves us and has freed us from our sins by his blood, 6 and has made us to be a kingdom and priests to serve his God and Father—to him be glory and power for ever and ever! Amen.* Revelation 1:5b-6 NIV

In losing their priestly role, Israel was losing their divine purpose.

Loss of Contentment

> *"They will eat but not have enough;*
>   *they will engage in prostitution but not flourish,*
> *because they have deserted the Lord* Hosea 4:10a NIV

Their pursuits left them without satisfaction. Greed and selfishness never satisfy because no amount of material gain ever feels like enough. They pursued items incapable of satisfying.

> *My people consult a wooden idol,*
>   *and a diviner's rod speaks to them.* Hosea 4:12a NIV

False worship can promise all kinds of things. Still, it cannot deliver.

> *A spirit of prostitution leads them astray;*
>   *they are unfaithful to their God.* Hosea 4:12b NIV

While their practice of pagan worship likely included temple prostitution, they were guilty of literal prostitution. But the emphasis here is spiritual prostitution, unfaithfulness to God Himself.

Loss of the Next Generation

*Therefore your daughters turn to prostitution
  and your daughters-in-law to adultery.* Hosea 4:13b NIV

While there are exceptions, this general rule often is true: *The apple does not tend to fall far from the tree.* A friend recently reminded me of Harry Chapin's song *Cats in the Cradle*. He noted the older he gets, the more this song scared him. Israel should be frightened about the trajectory their rebellion set for their children.

Loss of Family

*"Though you, Israel, commit adultery,
  do not let Judah become guilty.
"Do not go to Gilgal;
  do not go up to Beth Aven.
And do not swear, 'As surely as the Lord lives!'* Hosea 4:15 NIV

People do not live in a vacuum. Our actions influence others beyond our immediate family. God warned Israel (the northern ten tribes of the Hebrews) not to hinder the devotion of Judah (the southern two tribes of the Hebrews).

Beth Aven translates *House of Wickedness*. It was a derogatory name for *Bethel*: House of God. Bethel was about 11 miles north of Jerusalem and stood at the border of Israel and Judah. The location had a reverent history in the Old Testament. In Hosea's time it became associated with the worship of pagan deities rather than the one true God.

JUDGMENT

The verdict is in! This chapter begins with a word of condemnation to the priests.

"Hear this, you priests!
 Pay attention, you Israelites!
Listen, royal house!
 This judgment is against you: Hosea 5:1 NIV

Now comes the sentencing upon the people:

Withdrawal of God

When they go with their flocks and herds
 to seek the Lord,
they will not find him;
 he has withdrawn himself from them. Hosea 5:6 NIV

The verb *withdrawn* is the verb used most commonly among English translations. Our theology states this truth: *sin separates us from God.* The idea of God's absence <u>should</u> make us shudder. Spending eternity void of God's presence is an apt description of hell itself. Jesus came to *bridge* this separation through His death on the cross.

Destruction

Ephraim will be laid waste
 on the day of reckoning.
Among the tribes of Israel
 I proclaim what is certain. Hosea 5:9 NIV

In 722 BC, Assyria destroyed Israel. Hosea's prophecy was fulfilled within a few decades of his message.

Isolation

"When Ephraim saw his sickness,
 and Judah his sores,
then Ephraim turned to Assyria,
 and sent to the great king for help.
But he is not able to cure you,
 not able to heal your sores. Hosea 5:13 NIV

Ephraim was the name of one of the northern tribes of Israel and often served as a nickname for the entire nation. Instead of turning to the Lord for help, Israel looked to the king of Assyria. They needed prayer and true repentance. Instead, they trusted politics and treaties. Humanity's help felt more reliable than God's supply. Not only was the king of Assyria *not able to heal* their sores, they also became the nation who destroyed Israel, took their land, and carried their population into captivity.

APPEAL

In a courtroom, an *appeal* is a request for a more favorable judgment or for leniency. But in this case, the *appeal* is made not to the Lord but to the citizens of Israel.

The Request

"Come, let us return to the Lord.
He has torn us to pieces
 but he will heal us;
he has injured us

but he will bind up our wounds. Hosea 6:1 NIV

Hope and healing are found in their return to the Lord. However, their lighthearted attitude toward God appears in the next two verses.

2 After two days he will revive us;
    on the third day he will restore us,
    that we may live in his presence.
3 Let us acknowledge the Lord;
    let us press on to acknowledge him.
As surely as the sun rises,
    he will appear;
he will come to us like the winter rains,
    like the spring rains that water the earth." Hosea 6:2-3 NIV

The request, which first looked genuine or sincere, actually was shallow and empty. Israel was looking for a quick fix, a temporary bandage. Toward this end, they presumed upon God like a "vending machine" bound to respond hastily in the way they desired.

The Rejection

Sometimes God answers "no" to our prayers. In this case, God says "no" to their insincere repentance.

4 "What can I do with you, Ephraim?
    What can I do with you, Judah? Hosea 6:4a NIV

My Old Testament college professor, Dr. Don Garner, compared this verse to the words of an exasperated parent who has given a rebellious child every advantage and opportunity. *What more can I do than what I have done?*

Your love is like the morning mist,
  like the early dew that disappears. Hosea 6:4b NIV

God knew their love was temporary and fleeting. One of my favorite adages describing superficial devotion declares, *If it fizzles at the finish it was flawed from the first.* God knew their love was flawed and incapable of lasting.

The Reason

The reason their appeal was rejected was because Israel lacked evidence of a truly changed heart:

For I desire mercy, not sacrifice,
  and acknowledgment of God rather than burnt offerings.
Hosea 6:6 NIV

They went through the outward actions of making sacrifices in worship. But mercy toward the disadvantaged was lacking. In reality, the person who does not sacrifice probably will not have mercy. Genuine devotion to the Lord results in the presence of both mercy AND sacrifice.

Christians should note the phrase *I desire mercy, not sacrifice,* is quoted by Jesus twice in Matthew's gospel affirming God's true designs for us. The first time is in Matthew 9:13 when Jesus was asked why He ate with tax collectors and sinners. Jesus quoted it again in Matthew 12:7 in response to the Pharisee's accusations he violated the Sabbath.

The Israelites needed to ponder this question: *Do you want to be rescued from the consequences of your sins or from your sins?* The answer to this question reveals how genuine our repentance is.

I recently saw a sermon on this chapter entitled: <u>*Day of Decision or Hour of Intent*</u>. Israel's devotion and repentance may have contained some redeemable *intentions*. However, the blending of mere good intentions, rebellious actions, and feeble decisions resulted in a most disappointing "day in court."

10 – HOSEA
Chapters 7 - 10
A Series of Similes

My high school English teacher was a brilliant lady named Mildred Dupree. I credit her with teaching me the definition of a *simile*: A *simile* is a figure of speech involving the comparison of one thing with another thing of a different kind. It is used to describe items more emphatically. Common examples include:
- *as brave as a lion*
- *as crazy as a fox*
- *as skinny as a rail*
- *as big as a house*

In this third lesson from Hosea our attention turns to chapters 7-10. Having found Israel guilty of disloyalty and disobedience to the Lord, Hosea incorporated a series of ten similes to compare Israel's waywardness to numerous items. Specifically, Israel is like….

A BAND OF THIEVES

They practice deceit,
 thieves break into houses,
 bandits rob in the streets;
2 but they do not realize
 that I remember all their evil deeds.
Their sins engulf them;
 they are always before me.. Hosea 7:1b-2 NIV

Typically, thieves do not wish to be seen doing their evil deeds. But as a thief, Israel practiced their plunder *in the streets* for all to see. Ironically, they were the ones blind to the wickedness in their own hearts. In addition, they failed to realize how God always observes their sins.

Imagine a child goes against his parent"s instructions and plunders cookies from the cookie jar. He may deny performing this insubordinate deed, but his face covered in crumbs tells the true story. Many folks are blind to or dismissive of their own wrongdoings. But God remembers all their wickedness. Their evil deeds are obvious and observable right in front of God's face.

A HOT OVEN

Their hearts are like an oven;
 they approach him with intrigue.
Their passion smolders all night;
 in the morning it blazes like a flaming fire. Hosea 7:6 NIV

There is nothing "mild" about their wrongs. There was intensity to their rebellion.

In earlier times, preparing a meal took a great amount of intentional preparation. To cook a hot meal in the morning meant a fire had to start the night before. In time, the smoldering temperature became intense. In Israel's case, the heat was destructive.

All of them are hot as an oven;
 they devour their rulers.
All their kings fall,
 and none of them calls on me. Hosea 7:7 NIV

Kings and dynasties fell in the fervor of their heated rebellion. At one point in their timeline, Israel had five kings in thirteen years. Overall, Israel experienced nine different dynasties after their division from Judah.

A HALF-BAKED LOAF

> *"Ephraim mixes with the nations;*
> *Ephraim is a flat loaf not turned over..* Hosea 7:8 NIV

The nomadic people of the Middle East baked their bread on hot rocks. If the dough wasn't turned regularly, one side of the loaf would burn while the other side was uncooked.

A friend recently told me about attending a "tailgate" event where folks made pizza in specially designed outdoor ovens. Each pizza was regularly turned so it would cook evenly. Because of their compromising posture, Israel was "burned" by Assyria on one side. Meanwhile, their lack of devotion to the Lord left them uncooked on the other side.

People often are overly passionate about inferior things and not passionate enough about holy things. As a pastor, I often wish folks showed as much devotion to the Lord as they do to finances, leisure, schedules, fandom, habits, and many other distractions.

The gracious work of the Lord must permeate our entire being. Yet this is a goal in which we ALL fall short.

AN AGING PERSON

> *Foreigners sap his strength,*
> *but he does not realize it.*
> *His hair is sprinkled with gray,*
> *but he does not notice.*
> *10 Israel's arrogance testifies against him,*
> *but despite all this*
> *he does not return to the Lord his God*
> *or search for him* Hosea 7:9-10 NIV

Finish this sentence: *I used to be able to....*

Your particular conclusion to this statement may refer to physical actions, mental abilities, or any number of activities which declined due to age. Of course, these regressions do not occur suddenly, but gradually. Hosea noted such strength diminishes so slowly we may not notice it. In our pride we may simply refuse to admit it. At sixty-four years old, I sometimes look in the mirror and do not recognize the old man looking back at me. Indeed, often people forget how old they really are and behave foolishly. (My dad and I routinely warn each other against climbing ladders.)

Israel weakened to a point where their ways no longer worked. Still, the people failed to note their decline, to return to the Lord, and to search after Him.

A SENSELESS BIRD

"Ephraim is like a dove,
 easily deceived and senseless—
now calling to Egypt,
 now turning to Assyria.
12 When they go, I will throw my net over them;
 I will pull them down like the birds in the sky.
When I hear them flocking together,
 I will catch them.. Hosea 7:11-12 NIV

First, Israel "flew" south to Egypt for help. Then they "flew" north to Assyria. But neither nation proved to be a true ally. Their flying from one place to another eventually got them caught in God's net.

It is one thing to trade and share commerce with other nations, but the Hebrews were not to make alliances which would compromise their obedience to the Lord. Remember, Solomon entered many marriages to foreign wives as part of alliances with other nations. But a downfall came when these wives introduced their pagan worship to the Hebrews and led the nation to neglect the Lord. To borrow Hosea's word, it was a *senseless* strategy.

A TRECHEROUS BOW

They do not turn to the Most High;
they are like a faulty bow.
Their leaders will fall by the sword
because of their insolent words.
For this they will be ridiculed
in the land of Egypt.. Hosea 7:16a NIV

"Bow" here refers to a bow and arrow. Most translations describe the "bow" as *deceitful*. Terms such as *faulty, crooked, poorly crafted,* and *treacherous* are in other translations.

Because they strayed from the Lord, gave insincere repentance, and relied upon other powers, they could not "shoot straight." Israel would not win the battle. Even an expert archer cannot hit his or her target with a faulty bow.

AN EAGLE

Put the trumpet to your lips! Hosea 8:1a NIV

During Old Testament times, the Hebrews used a trumpet to announce special occasions, sound alarms, or give call for people to gather. Today, in certain communities, there are sirens and warnings of dangers (tornado, fire, etc). Here the sound of the trumpet called to signal an alert because the enemy was coming.

> *An eagle is over the house of the Lord*
> *because the people have broken my covenant*
> *and rebelled against my law.* Hosea 8:b NIV

We admire eagles and marvel at seeing them in flight. But for much of the animal kingdom, an eagle is a predator. An Assyrian eagle was about to swoop down and destroy Israel because they broke God's covenant through their idolatry, injustice, and paganism. Israel rebelled against the only one who could help them. They went their own way and manufactured their own gods who offered nothing.

EMPTY SOWING AND REAPING

> *"They sow the wind*
> *and reap the whirlwind.*
> *The stalk has no head;*
> *it will produce no flour.*
> *Were it to yield grain,*
> *foreigners would swallow it up.* Hosea 8:7 NIV

Through their idolatry and political alliances Israel was trying to "sow seeds" that would create a good harvest. But instead, they sowed into nothing and reaped only the "whirlwind." They threw "their seed" away to sources which could not deliver produce.

During this time, Israel's most common false deities were Baal and Asherah. These "gods" were supposed to bring good harvests and fruitfulness. But the stalk brought no harvest. Even if it did yield grain, their enemies would "swallow it up."

Putting forth a lot of effort without any favorable results is a formula for frustration. No one wants to sacrifice great amounts of work and have empty results. Still, this dynamic was their future. Consider things people try today which deliver very little in return.

A WANDERING DONKEY

For they have gone up to Assyria
like a wild donkey wandering alone. Hosea 8:9a NIV

Israel was like a dumb animal lost in the wilderness. Having forsaken her God, she was now forsaken by other nations and would face a terrible future on her own. One of life's hardest and saddest situations is to be and feel "alone."

Technically they were not without other people. But they isolated themselves away from the Lord. Here was a time when God would say to them, *Thy will be done,* allowing them to wander their own way.

A TRAINED HEIFER

Ephraim is a trained heifer
  that loves to thresh;
so I will put a yoke
  on her fair neck.
I will drive Ephraim,
  Judah must plow,
  and Jacob must break up the ground.
12 Sow righteousness for yourselves,
  reap the fruit of unfailing love,

> and break up your unplowed ground;
>   for it is time to seek the Lord,
> until he comes
>   and showers his righteousness on you. Hosea 10:11-12 NIV

Threshing is separating the grain from a plant. It was work done after harvesting the crops. Hosea said the Israelites liked the abundant fruit, but neglected the plowing and planting which was necessary beforehand. It is something like an employee who loves to go to work on payday but negligent about showing up any other time. Now Israel must go about plowing. In fact, their fate was not just plowing but plowing *unplowed* ground: hard, fallow, uncultivated, and packed dirt.

CONCLUSION:

Like other prophets, Hosea often utilized poetry in his messages. Characteristically, poetry tends to be repetitive. Chapters 10 and 11 review a few familiar "choruses."

You Have Mistreated God's Message and Messenger-

> *Because your sins are so many*
>   *and your hostility so great,*
> *the prophet is considered a fool,*
>   *the inspired person a maniac.*
> *8 The prophet, along with my God,*
>   *is the watchman over Ephraim,*
> *yet snares await him on all his paths,*
>   *and hostility in the house of his God.* Hosea 9:7b-8 NIV

In an earlier lesson, I quoted my Old Testament Professor, Don Garner. Another statement I remember Dr. Garner saying is: *If God calls you to be a prophet, be a prophet. But remember what they did to the prophets!* Hosea noted God's prophets were considered fools and maniacs.

Often, what we want to hear and what we need to hear are different things. When you hear a message you do not wish to hear, do you easily dismiss the message and/or the messenger? While our modern access to so much information has great benefits, it also means we can find (and follow) only messages saying what we personally want to hear. I recently read a phrase describing the challenge for someone genuinely looking for accurate and authentic truth in the midst of contemporary media: *Filter out the nonsense.* Find and follow the truth even when it is inconvenient.

Dealing Poorly with Prosperity

Remember, in the early part of the 8th century BC, Israel's economy was strong. Commerce was good. Hosea gave a summary of their history, focusing on their current prosperity and its devastating aftermath.

Israel was a spreading vine;
 he brought forth fruit for himself.
As his fruit increased,
 he built more altars;
as his land prospered,
 he adorned his sacred stones.
2 Their heart is deceitful,
 and now they must bear their guilt.
The Lord will demolish their altars
 and destroy their sacred stones. Hosea 10:1-2 NIV

A Long Walk with the Minor Prophets

> *The high places of wickedness will be destroyed—*
> *it is the sin of Israel.*
> *Thorns and thistles will grow up*
> *and cover their altars.* Hosea 10:8a NIV

Historically, people are more religious in times of hardship than in seasons of prosperity. Culturally, wealthy people are less active in faith than those impoverished. If God grants you wealth, be diligent, less the object of your confidence transition toward your money and away from the Lord. Hosea notes how these alternate sources of security eventually will decline.

There is Hope

> *Sow righteousness for yourselves,*
> *reap the fruit of unfailing love,*
> *and break up your unplowed ground;*
> *for it is time to seek the Lord,*
> *until he comes*
> *and showers his righteousness on you.* Hosea 10:12 NIV

Things were bad, but it was possible for them to get better. I am a native of Knoxville, Tennessee and was born within view of Neyland Stadium where the University of Tennessee plays football. My dad pointed out this observation: *No matter how bad things are going for the Vols, their fanbase always hopes and believes it is going to get better.* Devotion to the Lord was going bad for Israel. But Hosea notes it could get better.

Toward the end of Charles Dickins' *A Christmas Carol* the Ghost of Christmas Future shows Ebenezer Scrooge the sadness of his impending story. Scrooge would perish forgotten and unloved. His belongings would be cast off.

Those people associated with them would continue in deep grief and hardship. Shown the ominous road ahead, Scrooge asks: *Are these the shadows of the things that Will be, or are they shadows of the things that May be only?*

Hosea affirms the difficult prophecies of Israel are not necessarily *things that Will be*, but *the things May be* if the people repent and sow righteousness. There is hope!

11 – HOSEA
Chapters 11 - 14
Love Works

Albert C. Fisher lived from 1886 to 1946. His noteworthy life accomplishments include completing a Doctor of Divinity degree from Asbury College in Kentucky and serving as a military chaplain during World War 1. But Dr. Fisher primarily is remembered as a hymn writer. He even edited a hymnal, *Best Revival Songs*, published in 1924. Among his many hymns, the one I know best is *Love is the Theme*. I remember singing it in church during my childhood. It is sung to a solid military-like tempo.

Of the themes that men have known,
One supremely stands alone;
Through the ages it has shown,
'Tis His wonderful, wonderful love.
Chorus:
Love is the theme, love is supreme;
Sweeter it grows, glory bestows;
Bright as the sun ever it glows!
Love is the theme, eternal theme!

Many years ago, my father preached an illustration of a family who routinely shared family devotions in the evening. Each night a different child was called on to read a short passage out of the family Bible. One night the preschool-aged son asked to read the scripture. Even though he was not yet old enough to read, he proudly took the Bible, opened it to a random page, pointed his finger at the print and said, "God is love." He then turned a few pages and again pointed down saying, "God is love." His older siblings were about to tease him about his actions. But the father redeemed the moment by affirming to the family this truth: Every page of the Bible carries that same message: *God is love.*

Indeed, love IS the theme! Love is the theme of the Bible AND love is the theme of Hosea's closing chapters.

CHARACTERISTICS OF GOD'S LOVE

In our previous study, Hosea used similes comparing Israel to ten different images. These included a loaf of bread, an aging person, and a senseless bird. Here, Hosea compared God's similarity to a parent's love toward a small child.

God's Love Is Compassionate

When Israel was a child, I loved him,
*   and out of Egypt I called my son.*
2 But the more they were called,
*   the more they went away from me.*
They sacrificed to the Baals
*   and they burned incense to images.*
3 It was I who taught Ephraim to walk,
*   taking them by the arms;*
but they did not realize
*   it was I who healed them.*
4 I led them with cords of human kindness,
*   with ties of love.*
To them I was like one who lifts
*   a little child to the cheek,*
*   and I bent down to feed them.* Hosea 11:1-4 NIV

This passage recognizes a couple of observations about this parent-child dynamic.

- **A small child can divert from the path a parent sets for him/her.**

But the more they were called,
the more they went away from me. Hosea 11:2b NIV

Over time, Israel's relationship to God routinely declined. Though continually called by God, their devotion digressed further and further away from Him. Children can be happy to receive a parent's gifts, but still not want to obey the giver. Likewise, the Hebrews enjoyed the idea of being God's chosen and elect, but they did not want to live in faithfulness to the Lord. Through their calling, Israel received something exceptionally valuable. Sadly, they did not care for it as they should.

- **A small child cannot appreciate the sacrifice a loving parent makes for him/her.**

This is true even for good children. Kids are simply too young to realize the sacrifices made for them by their parents. Hosea says the same about the lack of appreciation Israel has for the Lord's help.

but they did not realize
it was I who healed them. Hosea 11:3b NIV

In his beginning chapters, Hosea's story portrayed Israel like an unfaithful spouse. Here, Israel is like an oblivious and/or ungrateful son. If a child fails to see and appreciate the sacrifices an earthly parent makes, how much less can a child of God see and recognize the sacrifices made by a divine parent unless he/she believes boldly in faith.

Remember, we are all prone to be like Israel: Enjoying God's blessings while taking God for granted.

God's Love Is Patient

"Will they not return to Egypt
and will not Assyria rule over them
because they refuse to repent?
6 A sword will flash in their cities;
it will devour their false prophets
and put an end to their plans.
7 My people are determined to turn from me.
Even though they call me God Most High,
I will by no means exalt them. Hosea 11:5-7 NIV

God could have destroyed the nation for their disobedience. Instead, He chose to be long-suffering. He allowed them to go astray through their own rebellious ways and experience consequences for their sin. This providential plan required patience until the Hebrews came to a point of repentance. Peter puts it this way in his second epistle:

The Lord is not slow in keeping his promise, as some understand slowness. Instead he is patient with you, not wanting anyone to perish, but everyone to come to repentance. 2 Peter 3:9 NIV

First Corinthians 13 is known as "The Love Chapter" in the Bible. When Paul dictated how love behaves, the first quality he stated was "Love is Patient." God's love suffered long throughout the time Israel lost their freedom and their "exalted" status.

God's Love Is Committed

In the early 1900's George Matheson composed a hymn that opens with this line: *O love that will not let me go.* God, like a loving parent, cannot *let go* of His children.

"How can I give you up, Ephraim?
 How can I hand you over, Israel?
How can I treat you like Admah?
 How can I make you like Zeboyim?
My heart is changed within me;
 all my compassion is aroused.
9 I will not carry out my fierce anger,
 nor will I devastate Ephraim again.
For I am God, and not a man—
 the Holy One among you. Hosea 11:8-9a

Israel had no "right" to be protected or loved. But God's compassion was aroused to hold off their total devastation.

Notice the phrase *For I am God… the Holy One.* As God, He was true to His identity. He did not act as a human. Rather, He held to His covenant even as the Hebrews forsook their pledge.

The Hebrews failed to keep their covenant
 Ephraim has surrounded me with lies,
  Israel with deceit.
 And Judah is unruly against God,
  even against the faithful Holy One. Hosea 11:12
NIV

This is the distinction between a *covenant* as compared to a *contract*. When one party in a *contract* breaks the terms of an agreement, the other party no longer is obligated to their part of the arrangement. By comparison, a party in a *covenant* keeps his/her promise even when the other party fails to honor his/her duties.

Remember, God's compassion, patience, and commitment are all part of His grand plan for our salvation. God gave His innocent and only Son to suffer for the sins of the world. Jesus' death illustrates God's compassion, patience, and commitment we so desperately need.

ACCEPT NO SUBSTITUTES

Substitutes for God's love simply do not work. However, this truth does not keep people from trying them!

Ephraim feeds on the wind;
 he pursues the east wind all day
 and multiplies lies and violence. Hosea 12:1a NIV

The word for *feeds* means *grazes*. Imagine a hungry sheep ignoring the grass around him and chewing the wind instead. The idea is ridiculous. But this is the way the Hebrews were living. They looked for sustenance and meaning in things other than the Lord.

Alliances Do Not Work

He makes a treaty with Assyria
 and sends olive oil to Egypt. Hosea 12:1b NIV

Assyria and Egypt were large and powerful countries. Rather than trusting the Lord's protection, the Hebrews sought treaties sending the wealth of Israel to their adversaries. A treaty encouraging the sale and trade of goods stimulates commerce and economic wealth. Still, the ultimate source of security and treasure was the Lord alone. Do not expect any other person, power, or ally to do what God alone can do.

Dishonesty Does Not Work

At the beginning of the chapter Hosea mentioned the people's *lies and violence*. But these iniquities were not the end of their corruption. Stealing was abundant too:

The merchant uses dishonest scales
 and loves to defraud. Hosea 12:7 NIV

Swindling people can make you wealthy, but it certainly does not make you right with God. Rather than resulting in a comfortable lifestyle, the Lord says their destiny will be the opposite of the prosperity they pursued.

I will make you live in tents again,
 as in the days of your appointed festivals. Hosea 12:9b NIV

In Old Testament days, wealth often was held in real estate. God eventually will cause them to live like nomads in tents, as people without land. Soon, when the Assyrians defeated Israel, the Hebrews journeyed into exile in tents. The reference to *appointed festivals* referred to the Festival of Tabernacles which took place annually in late September. During this week, the Hebrews lived in tents on their property as a reminder of the time Moses and their ancestors traveled through the wilderness living in tents. This festival gave Israel a brief sampling of this lifestyle. But soon, it would become their daily existence.

Idolatry Does Not Work

Now they sin more and more;
 they make idols for themselves from their silver,
cleverly fashioned images,
 all of them the work of craftsmen. Hosea 13:2 NIV

The Hebrews abandoned Jehovah for Baal and his idols. However, this brought only spiritual emptiness. While folks today do not tend to fashion crafted images to worship, people can still grant ultimate value to things that are not ultimate. Some possible examples include power, leisure, work, wealth, family, recreation, and hobbies.

LOVE WORKS

Hosea expounded on how love works through a variety of dynamics.

As Discipline

The people of Samaria must bear their guilt,
 because they have rebelled against their God. Hosea 13:16 NIV

The people had to endure some consequences for their rebellion. Remember, a judge who never punishes a criminal is not a good judge but a bad

A Long Walk with the Minor Prophets

judge. A parent who never disciplines a child is not a good parent but a bad parent. When I was a boy, I did not get punished for every wrong I committed. Still, I was disciplined enough to know my parents lovingly set and enforced proper boundaries for me. The wages of sin is sin and there is destruction left in its wake.

God had shown Israel love in the past by delivering them from Egypt. He gave them a home in the Promised Land. He provided for them. And He allowed them to be an established nation. Now the Lord demonstrated them love through their experience of discipline.

As Repentance

Repentance is an essential way for people to show love to the Lord. Hosea spoke to Israel like parents speak to little children, telling them just what to do.

Return, Israel, to the Lord your God.
  Your sins have been your downfall!
2 Take words with you
  and return to the Lord.
Say to him:
  "Forgive all our sins
and receive us graciously,
  that we may offer the fruit of our lips.
3 Assyria cannot save us;
  we will not mount warhorses.
We will never again say 'Our gods'
  to what our own hands have made,
    for in you the fatherless find compassion." Hosea 14:1-4 NIV

Responsible parents commonly provide their small children with conciliatory words to say when they commit a wrong. With a vocal "nudge" the proper expression is extended such as, *Say you are sorry*. This is what the prophet told Israel to do. This is what Israel needed to do!

As Healing

On rare occasions, healing is instantaneous. But this is exceptional. Healing tends to be an extended process. The Hebrews did not suddenly fall into their terrible problems. Getting stuck in the deep consequences of sin was the result of a long, gradual decline. Similarly, God says their healing would be prolonged.

4 "I will heal their waywardness
  and love them freely,
  for my anger has turned away from them.
5 I will be like the dew to Israel;
  he will blossom like a lily.
Like a cedar of Lebanon
  he will send down his roots;
6   his young shoots will grow.
His splendor will be like an olive tree,
  his fragrance like a cedar of Lebanon.
7 People will dwell again in his shade;
  they will flourish like the grain, **Hosea 14:4-7a NIV**

Once again, the prophet utilized the literary tool of similes. God will be *like the dew* that causes flowers to bloom. Israel, on the other hand, is compared to two types of trees: *a cedar of Lebanon* and *an olive tree*. The cedar of Lebanon was well-regarded and well-respected in ancient times. Solomon used cedars of

Lebanon in the construction of the first temple (1 King 5:6). Note the reference to their roots. Time is required for a tree to dig to such deep depths. Olive trees are known for their longevity. They can live beyond 1000 years. Israel becoming such a tree would take many seasons of maturity.

Often there is a period of recuperation for people to return to strength and restore their appetite for spiritual food. But, rest assured, healing does come around.

As Wisdom

Who is wise? Let them realize these things.
  Who is discerning? Let them understand.
The ways of the Lord are right;
  the righteous walk in them,
  but the rebellious stumble in them. Hosea 14:9 NIV

Hosea closed his prophecy with an appeal to those folks who were *wise* and *discerning*. Such individuals understand a situation and respond properly. In the end, people in Hosea's day (and in our day) are called to recognize the two choices before them and choose prudently:

> rebel against the Lord and stumble, or
> return to the Lord and walk securely in His ways.

The wise choice is the loving choice.

The old hymn was right: *Love IS the Theme.* Love is the theme of Hosea's prophecy and the theme of the entirety of scripture.

*For God so **loved** the world that he gave his one and only Son, that whoever believes in him shall not perish but have eternal life.* John 3:16 NIV

*God demonstrates his own **love** for us in this: While we were still sinners, Christ died for us.* Romans 5:8 NIV

*8Whoever does not love does not know God, for God is **love**. 9God's **love** was revealed among us in this way: God sent his only Son into the world so that we might live through him.* 1 John 4:8-9 NRSV

GOMER by Jeff Mowery

Sung to the tune of *Ruby, Don't Take Your Love to Town* written by Mel Tillis and recorded by Waylon Jennings, Johnny Darrell, and Kenny Rogers.

You've painted up your lips and left me for some other men.
Gomer, are you contemplating leaving me again?
The rumor on the street tells me your love is fading down.
O Gomer, don't take your love to town.

The Lord told me to go and take a wife of harlotry.
Because His people went and loved some pagan deities.
And yes, it's true, I'm not the man that God's called me to be.
O Gomer, I still want your company.

God gave us children and He gave them very funny names
To show the people that their sin was causing their great shame
Turn to the Lord and maybe His great wrath will not come down
O Gomer, don't take your love to town.

I made a promise to the Lord that I would buy you back.
And even though, like Israel, your heart was very black.
Repent and turn unto the Lord and Yes, you will be found!!!
O Gomer, don't take your love to town.

O Gomer, for God's sake, turn around!!!

A Long Walk with the Minor Prophets

A Long Walk with the Minor Prophets

12 – MICAH
Chapters 1 - 2
You Have Been Warned

In our previous lesson Hosea closed his writing with a call for discernment:
> *Who is wise? Let them realize these things.*
> *Who is discerning? Let them understand.* Hosea 14:9a NIV

In this study we find an answer to Hosea's question: Micah is discerning! God gave him insight into the changes on the horizon for Israel and Judah along with the wisdom to respond appropriately.

INTRODUCTION

As the chart below shows, Micah lived in a challenging time. During his ministry the nation of Israel fell to the Assyrians and Judah continued to decline.

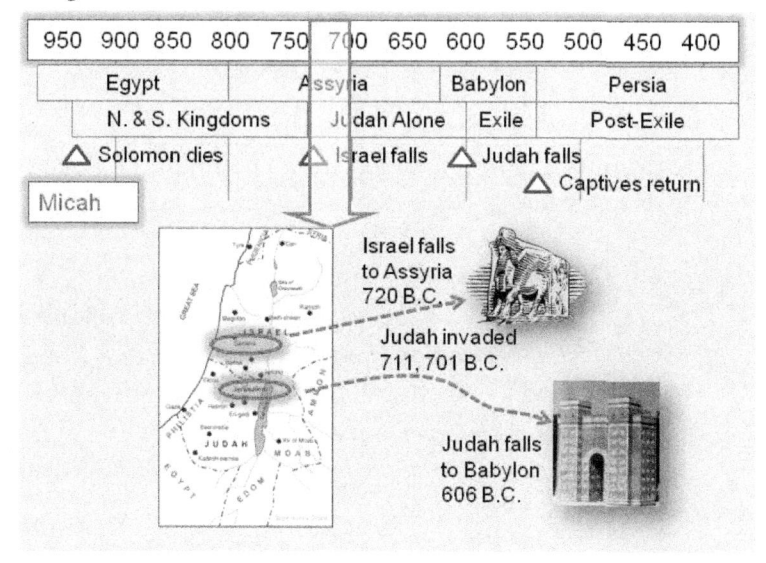

950	900	850	800	750	700	650	600	550	500	450	400
Egypt				Assyria			Babylon		Persia		
N. & S. Kingdoms				Judah Alone			Exile		Post-Exile		

△ Solomon dies   △ Israel falls   △ Judah falls   △ Captives return

Micah

Israel falls to Assyria 720 B.C.
Judah invaded 711, 701 B.C.
Judah falls to Babylon 606 B.C.

The Prophet

This book of prophecy begins with a basic introduction to the prophet himself:

The word of the Lord that came to Micah of Moresheth during the reigns of Jotham, Ahaz and Hezekiah, kings of Judah— the vision he saw concerning Samaria and Jerusalem. Micah 1:1 NIV

Micah's name means "Who is like Jehovah?" It affirms the unique holiness of the Lord. His hometown of Moresheth was located about 25 miles southwest of Jerusalem.

Micah's prophetic role lasted from about 735 B.C. to 700 B.C. During Micah's ministry, Isaiah also preached to Judah while Amos and Hosea prophesized to the north. We see that the prophets often overlapped in their ministries.

The Message

The book of Micah features three messages from the prophet. All three launch with a command to "hear" or to "listen":

- *Hear, you peoples, all of you,*
  listen, earth and all who live in it, Micah 1:2a NIV
- *"Listen, you leaders of Jacob, you rulers of Israel.* Micah 3:1a NIV
- *"Hear, you mountains, the Lord's accusation;*
  listen, you everlasting foundations of the earth. Micah 6:2a NIV

The first "sermon" is found in chapters 1 and 2. It is a message of warning to all the Hebrews.

YOU'VE BEEN WARNED: THE JUDGE IS COMING

My high school marching band director was an exceptional music teacher named Norman Woodall. In leading the band, Mr. Woodall did not put up with nonsense. Prior to the start of school, we spent a week at a local college participating in "band camp." During these days, we learned our marching show for the fall season. The bottom two floors on our dormitory were designated for girls and the top two floors were for the boys. Consequently, the dormitory stairwells became a popular evening hangout. One night a good number of us fellowshipped in the stairwells beyond curfew. The space was buzzing with enthusiastic teens. Suddenly, those of us on an upper landing noted a rapid stirring among our peers below. Looking over the handrail, I saw the stern face of Mr. Woodall appear as he steadily and quietly ascended the staircase. The authority had arrived, and we scrambled to our rooms.

Micah calls his audiences' attention to the arrival of the Lord, their ultimate authority. His entrance carries two qualities.

Powerfully

Look! The Lord is coming from his dwelling place;
  he comes down and treads on the heights of the earth.
4 The mountains melt beneath him
  and the valleys split apart,
like wax before the fire,
  like water rushing down a slope. Micah 1:3-4 NIV

One of the famous sermons of history was preached by Jonathan Edwards during America's colonial days: *Sinners in the Hands of an Angry God.* Micah's words gave the idea that the Lord was coming in an intimidating fashion. I recently described two college basketball coaches by saying they coached "angry." Their intensity especially showed when something in the game went counter to either coach's wishes. They too were like authoritative kings.

While our God is often portrayed as gentle and compassionate, He is vehemently opposed to our sin. I preached recently on Genesis 3 where Adam and Eve hid from God in the Garden of Eden. They were afraid of God. They knew He was holy. In contrast, they recognized their own sin. In that sermon I said, *If you have never encountered God in an intimidating way, you might consider whether you have created a God in your mind that is simply too comfortable.*

Personally

Here Micah started naming names! Remember, the prophet Amos opened his preaching by pointing out the sins of people from distant lands. But Micah names the names of his own people!

5 All this is because of Jacob's transgression,
  because of the sins of the people of Israel.
What is Jacob's transgression?
  Is it not Samaria?
What is Judah's high place?
  Is it not Jerusalem? Micah 1:3-5 NIV

Both Judah and Israel were guilty. Their hearts were not true to the Lord. I suspect, if these two cultures were asked, the residents of one nation would point to the other as the "unrighteous ones." But Micah said <u>both</u> were wrong. While sin exists outside the ranks of God's people, it also dwells **inside** God's own family. Peter wrote in his first epistle:

For the time is come that judgment must begin at <u>the house of God</u>. 1 Peter 4:17 KJV

Most people are fine with judgment just as long as they are not the ones being judged! But the great judge arrived to condemn the sins of all the Hebrew people.

YOU'VE BEEN WARNED: THE CONSEQUENCES ARE COMING

Micah continued with specific warnings to each nation. In these verses he emphasized the pending consequences of their wrongs.

To Israel

*"Therefore I will make Samaria a heap of rubble,
  a place for planting vineyards.
I will pour her stones into the valley
  and lay bare her foundations.
7 All her idols will be broken to pieces;
  all her temple gifts will be burned* Micah 1:6-7a NIV

Samaria's pagan religion involved idolatry and went against God's word. Thus, their pagan temple gifts were false and destined for destruction. God is a jealous God and unhappy when someone or something receives praise that should rightfully go to Him.

The destruction of Israel began in 722 BC. Many people in Israel were taken captive to Assyria. Later, Gentiles were relocated into Israel to live. When these immigrants intermarried with the Israelites left behind, they created a mixed race known in the New Testament as *Samaritans*.

To Judah

Micah described sin as terminal, contagious, and toxic.

For Samaria's plague is incurable;
 it has spread to Judah.
It has reached the very gate of my people,
 even to Jerusalem itself. Micah 1:9 NIV

The extent of their transgressions left them spiritually *incurable*, at least by human efforts. And although the *plague* of sin originated in Israel, the people of Judah are not off the hook. Simply saying, *They started it*, did not grant them clemency.

City Roll Call:

The remainder of this chapter details specific consequences to eleven cities. Micah used a clever series of puns based upon the names of cities. These names sound like what the enemy would do to the Hebrews. We will walk through these rather quickly.

Tell it not in Gath;
 weep not at all. Micah 1:10a

Gath is similar to the Hebrew word for *Tell*

Gath would not be "told." They were left out of the revelation of God's word.

In Beth Ophrah
roll in the dust. Micah 1:12

> **Beth Orphrah** means *House of dust.*
> These residents would be rolling in the dust of destruction.

11 Pass by naked and in shame,
you who live in Shaphir.

> **Shaphir** means *Pleasant* or *Beautiful.*
> Instead, people of Shaphir would look "naked" and far from beautiful in appearance.

Those who live in Zaanan
will not come out.

> **Zaanan** means *Come Out.*
> But their residents could not "come out" when they were a captured city.

Beth Ezel is in mourning;
it no longer protects you.

> **Beth Ezel** translates *House of taking away.*
> Soon, their own homes would be taken away.

12 Those who live in Maroth writhe in pain,
waiting for relief,
because disaster has come from the Lord,
even to the gate of Jerusalem.

> **Maroth** means *bitterness.*

They would writhe in bitter pain.

13 You who live in Lachish,
  harness fast horses to the chariot.
You are where the sin of Daughter Zion began,
  for the transgressions of Israel were found in you.

> **Lachish** sounds like the term for "team of swift horses." Their destruction would make them refugees, fleeing quickly while hotly pursued by their enemies.

14 Therefore you will give parting gifts
  to Moresheth Gath.

> **Moresheth** sounds like Hebrew for *betrothed*. Engaged couples typically expect wedding gifts. Now they give *parting gifts*.

The town of Akzib will prove deceptive
  to the kings of Israel.

> **Akzib** means *deception*
> Its people were deceived by idolatry and greed.

15 I will bring a conqueror against you
  who live in Mareshah.

> **Mareshah** sounds like the word for *conqueror*
> Instead, they were the ones conquered.

The nobles of Israel
  will flee to Adullam.

> **Adullam** was a town of the Canaanites allotted to Judah and lying in the lowlands. It was the site

154

of the cave where David hid. Soon, these residents would flee in hiding.

Micah closed this chapter with this summary description.

> *16 Shave your head in mourning*
> *for the children in whom you delight;*
> *make yourself as bald as the vulture,*
> *for they will go from you into exile.*

Sadly, even the little children were going into exile. Tragically, the innocent lives of these young ones suffered. It recently was reported that 50-70% of the casualties from the current warfare in the Middle East were women and children. This should make us sad because it makes God sad.

YOU'VE BEEN WARNED: YOUR SINS ARE MANY

Indeed, the Hebrew people were privileged. Still, privilege brings responsibility and accountability. Sometimes, in the midst of punishment, a person may cry out *What did I Do Wrong?* There is no need for that question here. Micah highlighted their sins.

Greed

> *Woe to those who plan iniquity,*
> *to those who plot evil on their beds!*
> *At morning's light they carry it out*
> *because it is in their power to do it.*
> *2 They covet fields and seize them,*
> *and houses, and take them.*
> *They defraud people of their homes,*
> *they rob them of their inheritance.* Micah 2:1-2 NIV

One of the primary measures of wealth in the biblical world was land ownership. Micah expresses "woe" (sadness) upon those who lie in bed planning ways to cheat others out of their fields and homes. Land barons were bent on acquiring large estates and monopolizing their holdings, while impoverishing others.

The **secular** version of *The Golden Rule* states: *Whoever has the gold makes the rules.* In contrast, Jesus taught us to not be consumed with acquiring even the necessities such as clothing and food. Rather, we are to…

> *Seek ye first the Kingdom of God and His righteousness. And all these things shall be added unto you.* Matthew 6:33.

In the Mosaic Law (Leviticus 25), land was to be returned to the original family owners every 50 years (The *Year of Jubilee*). This design discouraged monopolies of land ownership where the rich oppressed the poor.

False Prophecy

> *"Do not prophesy," their prophets say.*
> *"Do not prophesy about these things;*
> *disgrace will not overtake us."* Micah 2:6 NIV

False prophets were not keen on Micah's predictions of destruction and hardship. Instead, their message said, *We are God's people. He would not let these tragic things happen to us. We only want to hear positive things!*

But where God gives a promise there is also a premise. Notice the next verse:

Do not my words do good to the one whose ways are upright? Micah 2:7b NIV

God has designed the world for goodness to follow uprightness. These false prophets told the people what they wanted to hear: *Everything is good. Do whatever you wish.*

As a general rule, popular religion is false religion. Anyone can join the crowd. Going through the motions is not sincere religion. And a prophet whose message can be bought is a liar and deceiver.

If a liar and deceiver comes and says,
　'I will prophesy for you plenty of wine and beer,'
　　that would be just the prophet for this people! Micah 2:11 NIV

False prophets preached any subject the people wanted to hear, including a message promising the benefits of strong drink!

YOU'VE BEEN WARNED: BUT THERE IS HOPE

Warren Wiersbe's commentary on Micah includes this observation:

- *Conviction without hope creates only hopelessness.*

In spite of his sharp words, the prophet closes with a message of hope.

A Great Reunion Awaits

> *"I will surely gather all of you, Jacob;*
> *I will surely bring together the remnant of Israel.*
> *I will bring them together like sheep in a pen,*
> *like a flock in its pasture;*
> *the place will throng with people.* Micah 2:12 NIV

What declined into a remnant would rally into a *throng*! The word *throng* means *a noisy crowd, multitude,* or *many people.*

Can you be a faithful remnant? Will you be among the 20% of Christians who will do 80% of the ministry? Throughout most of its history, and in most of the world today, people who actively practice Christianity are in the small minority. But a day is coming when God's people will be beyond number:

> *After this I looked, and there before me was a great multitude that no one could count, from every nation, tribe, people and language, standing before the throne and before the Lamb. They were wearing white robes and were holding palm branches in their hands.* Revelation 7:9 NIV

A Great King Will Lead

> *The One who breaks open the way will go up before them;*
> *they will break through the gate and go out.*
> *Their King will pass through before them,*
> *the Lord at their head."* Micah 2:13 NIV

In the ancient world, kings returning from victorious military campaigns arrived home to a great parade and fanfare. Micah foresees a triumphant procession into the land with King Messiah at the head. The sentiment anticipates the hymn we sing during

> Advent: *Joy to the world the Lord has come. Let earth receive her King*! As Christians, we faithfully await the victorious return of King Jesus.

Until then, Micah's discernment commands us to be true to our great God and His ways. "Soft religion" rejects responsibility. "Soft religion" excuses expectations. "Soft religion" caters to our conveniences. "Soft religion" pampers our pride. True religion, however, inspires responsibility, devotion, compassion, and faithfulness.

13 – MICAH
Chapters 3 - 5
It Gets Worse Before It Gets Better

Most surgeries follow a general principle: *You have to get worse in order to get better.* The pain you experience recovering from surgery is part of the process toward a better physical condition than you knew before the surgery.

This study follows chapters 3-5 of Micah's prophecies. These chapters contain the second of his three sermons. While his previous sermon was a warning, this message looks to the future. Micah says to the Hebrews what we know when facing surgery: *It is going to get worse before it gets better.*

IT IS GOING TO GET WORSE BECAUSE LEADERS HAVE FAILED

In this world so much hinges on leadership! Sometimes I grieve because there are not more people willing to be a leader in God's work. However, Micah saw something even more difficult than NO leadership: POOR leadership.

Civil Leaders

Our previous lesson showed how Micah's three sermons all begin with a call to hear. This sermon directs the leaders of Judah and Israel to listen.

3 Then I said,
"Listen, you leaders of Jacob,
*   you rulers of Israel.*
Should you not embrace justice,
2   you who hate good and love evil;
who tear the skin from my people

> *and the flesh from their bones;*
> *3 who eat my people's flesh,*
>   *strip off their skin*
>   *and break their bones in pieces;*
> *who chop them up like meat for the pan,*
>   *like flesh for the pot?"* Micah 3:1-3 NIV

Micah condemned the destructive work of the Hebrew civil leadership. Their actions are gruesome and graphic. The role of government is to *embrace justice*, to protect and serve their constituents. These folks are making people victims! Civil leaders should be part of a society's solutions. Here, they were part of the problem.

> *4 Then they will cry out to the Lord,*
>   *but he will not answer them.*
> *At that time he will hide his face from them*
>   *because of the evil they have done.* Micah 3:4 NIV

At last, when these leaders called to the Lord, there was no answer. The opportunity was past. The words *It's too late* are some of the saddest words I know.

False Prophets

> *5 This is what the Lord says:*
> *"As for the prophets*
>   *who lead my people astray,*
> *they proclaim 'peace'*
>   *if they have something to eat,*
> *but prepare to wage war against anyone*
>   *who refuses to feed them.* Micah 3:5 NIV

These false prophets were not devoted to expressing truth. Instead, they told people what they wanted to

A Long Walk with the Minor Prophets

hear as long as they were well fed. Refuse to feed these "prophets" and they would "wage war."

6 Therefore night will come over you, without visions,
   and darkness, without divination.
The sun will set for the prophets,
   and the day will go dark for them.
7 The seers will be ashamed
   and the diviners disgraced.
They will all cover their faces
   because there is no answer from God." Micah 3:6-7 NIV

In the Old Testament some "prophets" were referred to as "seers." But in the spiritual darkness ahead, they will be unable to "see" at all.

In contrast to the false prophet, there is Micah:

8 But as for me, I am filled with power,
   with the Spirit of the Lord,
   and with justice and might,
to declare to Jacob his transgression,
   to Israel his sin. Micah 3:8 NIV

Micah proclaimed what the Hebrews needed to hear, not what they wanted to hear. It is a unique person who graciously and directly speaks of someone's wrongs.

Chapter three closes with Micah's blunt summary of their wrongs (5:9-11)

- They despise justice v. 9
- They build with bloodshed and wickedness v. 10
- They accept bribes. v. 11a

- They give false hope: *Is not the Lord among us? No disaster will come upon us."* v.11b

The words *It's your fault* also are among the saddest words I know. But this is what God says to the leaders of Israel and Judah:

12 Therefore <u>because of you</u>,
 Zion will be plowed like a field,
Jerusalem will become a heap of rubble,
 the temple hill a mound overgrown with thickets. 3:12

I am known around our church office for saying, *Nothing happens without a champion.* Ministry needs leaders who will "champion" various kingdom causes. Even now, God needs GOOD champions to carry out His will.

IT IS GOING TO GET BETTER IN THE LAST DAYS

The consequences of these misdeeds made things worse for Judah and Israel. But a day was coming when things would get better. Micah referred to this time as *the last days.*

In the last days Micah 4:1 NIV

> This is the great "day of the Lord" when God reigns completely and when all wrongs are made right. Therefore, when the *outlook* is grim, try the *uplook*. Here is an encouraging vision to see and follow.

See God's Promises

> These verses in Chapter 4 describe the world as God intended it to be and how it one day will be again. The Bible's descriptions of this reality are found in

the first two and last two chapters of the Bible. Here is what is promised:

- **Worship**

  the mountain of the LORD's temple will be established
  as the highest of the mountains;
  it will be exalted above the hills,
  and peoples will stream to it.
  ² Many nations will come and say
  "Come, let us go up to the mountain of the LORD,
  to the temple of the God of Jacob.
  He will teach us his ways,
  so that we may walk in his paths." Micah 4:1-2 NIV

  Revelation 22 describes the Tree of Life with these words:

  And the leaves of the tree are for the healing of the nations. Revelation 22:2b NIV

  In Micah's time, people of another nation (Assyria) were coming with their army to battle and destroy them. But a time was coming when all nations would desire to worship the Lord and walk in His path.

- **Justice**

  The law will go out from Zion,
  the word of the LORD from Jerusalem.
  ³ He will judge between many peoples
  and will settle disputes for strong nations far and wide.

The Lord Himself serves as the eternal judge capable of making sound judgments. Personally, I like that certain verdicts are left to God's wise judgment.

- **Peace**

*They will beat their swords into plowshares
and their spears into pruning hooks.
Nation will not take up sword against nation,
nor will they train for war anymore.* Micah 4:3b NIV

This is a great verse, envisioning a time when weapons of warfare are transformed into tools of productivity.

The amount society spends on items for "defense and protection" must be staggering. Consider the cost of Military, Law Enforcement, Firearms, Security Systems, Locks, Insurance, etc. According to the Congressional Budget Office website, about one-sixth of United States federal spending goes to national defense (-CBO Website). This amounts to a bit over 1 trillion dollars annually.

I am in full support of our armed forces and understand the necessity of their presence in a broken and fallen world. But one can dream of how lives and fortunes could benefit our world if today's *swords* could become *plowshares*.

- **Designation**

6 "In that day," declares the LORD,

> *"I will gather the lame;*
> *I will assemble the exiles*
> *and those I have brought to grief.*
> *⁷ I will make the lame my remnant,*
> *those driven away a strong nation.* Micah 4:6-7a NIV

The lame, exiles, and grieving were designated as God's "remnant." By definition, a remnant is a small remaining quantity of something. God's people may be a small minority. Still, they receive special designation. Remember, in most of history and in most of the world today, Christians are a minority, a remnant, of the greater population.

- **Endearment**

> *⁸ As for you, watchtower of the flock,*
> *stronghold of Daughter Zion,*
> *the former dominion will be restored to you;*
> *kingship will come to Daughter Jerusalem."* Micah 4:8 NIV

Of the elements we can draw from this verse, the expression *Daughter* is particularly meaningful. While these people have lived more like a rebellious child, the Lord uses this term of endearment twice in this verse to describe their relationship to Him.

Trust God's Working

> *¹⁰ Writhe in agony, Daughter Zion,*
> *like a woman in labor,*
> *for now you must leave the city*

> *to camp in the open field.*
> *You will go to Babylon;*
> *there you will be rescued.*
> *There the LORD will redeem you*
> *out of the hand of your enemies.* Micah 4:10 NIV

As a male, I admit to knowing little to nothing about labor pain. But I do know this: Out of the pain arrives a beautiful baby. Exile will be "agony" like a woman in labor. But a beautiful delivery of rescue and redemption awaits.

> *13 "Rise and thresh, Daughter Zion,*
> *for I will give you horns of iron;*
> *I will give you hooves of bronze,*
> *and you will break to pieces many nations."*
> *You will devote their ill-gotten gains to the LORD,*
> *their wealth to the Lord of all the earth.* Micah 4:13 NIV

God promises to create a strong and healthy nation. In Micah's imagery, *horns* are a symbol of power while *hooves* are a symbol of speed.

Your King is Coming

> *2 "But you, Bethlehem Ephrathah,*
> *though you are small among the clans of Judah,*
> *out of you will come for me*
> *one who will be ruler over Israel,*
> *whose origins are from of old,*
> *from ancient times."* Micah 5:2 NIV

Because it is quoted in Matthew's Christmas story, this may well be Micah's best-known verse. When the Magi came to Jerusalem in search of the newborn king, the chief priests and teachers of the law referenced this passage to point them to Bethlehem (Matthew 2:6). The future great king would be born in a humble village. *Ancient days* can be translated *eternal days*. This affirms the eternal divinity of the coming king.

THEREFORE, ENDURE TO THE END

In the late 1970's a Children's Musical named "God's Kids" by Rick and Sylvia Powell included a song about "Won't Be's" in heaven. Micah gave a list of both "will be's" and "won't be's" in the end times. Remembering these will help God's people endure through the time when things get worse.

Will Be's…

- **Security**

> *4 He will stand and shepherd his flock*
> *in the strength of the Lord,*
> *in the majesty of the name of the Lord his God.*
> *And they will live securely, for then his greatness*
> *will reach to the ends of the earth.* Micah 5:4 NIV

People thrive better in environments which are secure, stable, and safe from dangers.
In the end, we have security based on HIS greatness. As the hymn declares:

Safe and secure from all alarms. -Elisha Albright Hoffman (1839-1929)

- **Fruitfulness**

Like Hosea, Micah uses some similes to describe God's eternal people.

7 The remnant of Jacob will be
 in the midst of many peoples
like dew from the Lord,
 like showers on the grass,
which do not wait for anyone
 or depend on man. Micah 5:7 NIV

In a Middle East setting, dew and showers were essential for good agriculture. The remnant of Jacob will be like the moisture providing fertile productivity.

- **Strength**

The remnant of Jacob will be among the nations,
 in the midst of many peoples,
like a lion among the beasts of the forest,
 like a young lion among flocks of sheep, Micah 5:8a NIV

Like a young lion, the remnant will be powerful. Judah may be small, but it will deliver a great punch!

Won't Be's…

Micah turns attention to things which will be absent during the last days. Notice the many times the phrase *I will* appears. The Lord Himself makes them unnecessary.

- **Military Defenses**

10 "In that day," declares the Lord,
"I will destroy your horses from among you
 and demolish your chariots.
11 I will destroy the cities of your land
 and tear down all your strongholds. Micah 5:10-11 NIV

Because peace prevails, God destroys the weapons of warfare and the fortresses of defense. The third verse of the Marine Song features some good-hearted fun at the other branches of the military. It closes with these words:

If the army and the navy ever look at heaven's scenes.
They will find the streets are guarded by United States Marines.

No offense to the Marines or any of the Armed Forces, but they will not need to guard heaven. The Lord takes care of His kingdom.

- **Witchcraft**

    I will destroy your witchcraft
     and you will no longer cast spells. Micah 5:12 NIV

God eliminates dark religion which mocks and undermines true worship.

- **Idols**

    13 I will destroy your idols
     and your sacred stones from among you;
    you will no longer bow down
     to the work of your hands.
    14 I will uproot from among you your Asherah poles

when I demolish your cities. Micah 5:13-14 NIV

Throughout scripture, including the Second Commandment, God instructs humanity not to create idols. After all, nothing on earth can sufficiently represent the mightiness of the Lord. There will be no need for representations of God in heaven. We will be in the very presence of the Lord.

While times will get worse, Micah offers a favorable message regarding a positive outcome for the faithful. They can endure through the difficulties with assurance that things will get better.

During my seminary years, I pastored a small Baptist church in a southern Indiana town named Clearspring. Not long before my graduation, I officiated the funeral for a dear lady named Helen Brown. As part of her memorial service, the family asked me to sing an old hymn written in 1941 by Esther Kerr Rushoi. Even though I grew up in church, this was my first exposure to this song. The chorus gives a message of hope for those who remain faithful until things get better.

> *It will be worth it all when we see Jesus.*
> *Life's trials will seem so small when we see Christ.*
> *One look at his dear face, all sorrow will Erase.*
> *So bravely run the race, 'til we see Christ.*
> 						-Esther Kerr Rushoi

14 – MICAH
Chapters 6 - 7
Religious But Not Spiritual

I personally do not care to hear people describe themselves as "spiritual but not religious." This typically means they believe in God, Jesus, or certain doctrines. However, they do not engage with a community of believers. In addition, they are less likely to participate in any organized ministries. As a pastor I strive to formulate spiritual lives into meaningful religious structures.

The Hebrews in Micah's day were the opposite: They were *religious but not spiritual*. They practiced many outward expressions of spirituality. They listened to pleasant sounding prophets. They revered their temple buildings. But they had no heart for the Lord that translated into obedience and respect. They did what they wanted not what God wanted.

In our final lesson from Micah we come to the third of Micah's sermons.
- The first message was a warning.
- The second message condemned their leadership but expressed hope for the great Day of the Lord and their coming king.
- This third message is directed toward "the mountains" and takes on the character of a courtroom setting.

6 Listen to what the Lord says:
"Stand up, plead my case before the mountains;
    let the hills hear what you have to say. Micah 6:1 NIV

As in Micah's previous two sermons, this message begins with a call to "hear" or "listen." The beginning of a court session can open with the declaration: "Hear ye…Hear ye…"

The Lord presented His case against the Hebrews for their unfaithfulness. They were expected to be distinctive among the nations. The Law of Moses instructed them to live uniquely in how they ate, how they worked, how they governed themselves, and how they worshipped. Unfortunately, they lost much of their uniqueness by adopting the practices of surrounding nations and people.

Micah's final two chapters follow a pattern of accusation, punishment, and mercy.

THE CASE AGAINST THE PEOPLE

Accusation – They Forgot God's Goodness

Court opens with arguments presented against God's people.

2 "Hear, you mountains, the Lord's accusation;
listen, you everlasting foundations of the earth.
For the Lord has a case against his people;
he is lodging a charge against Israel.

Immediately, God calls up three historical witnesses testifying to the gracious ways the Lord had treated the Hebrews.

- **The Exodus**

3 "My people, what have I done to you?
How have I burdened you? Answer me.
4 I brought you up out of Egypt
and redeemed you from the land of slavery.

> *I sent Moses to lead you,*
>   *also Aaron and Miriam.* Micah 6:3-4 NIV

Perhaps the greatest intercession in their people's history was the Lord transforming the Hebrews from slaves into a people group and then into a nation. Certainly, God's hand brought this about.

- **Balaam's Blessings**

> *5 My people, remember*
>   *what Balak king of Moab plotted*
>   *and what Balaam son of Beor answered.* Micah 6:5a NIV

Three times Balka, King of Moab, commanded Balaam to curse Israel. But each time God turned the curse into a blessing (Numbers 22-24).

- **Crossing the Jordan**

> *Remember your journey from Shittim to Gilgal,*
>   *that you may know the righteous acts of the Lord."*
> Micah 6:5b NIV

Shittim and *Gilgal* reminded the Hebrews of the time God stopped the flow of the Jordan River so their ancestors could cross into the Promised Land (Joshua 3-4).

A proper response for these miraculous provisions should be loyalty to the Lord and His ways. Instead, the people of Israel and Judah followed selfish ambitions and false gods. The Lord was within His rights to challenge their rebellious behavior.

Their Response

Rather than confess their failings, the people of Micah's day considered what actions they could take to appease God's disappointment.

6 With what shall I come before the Lord
  and bow down before the exalted God?
Shall I come before him with burnt offerings,
  with calves a year old?
7 Will the Lord be pleased with thousands of rams,
  with ten thousand rivers of olive oil?
Shall I offer my firstborn for my transgression,
  the fruit of my body for the sin of my soul? Micah 6:6-7 NIV

In essence, they asked: "What will it take to *buy the Lord off?*" Each offer raised the bid: young calves, thousands of rams, ten thousand rivers of olive oil, and even child sacrifice.

But it is not the price that was the problem. Rather, it was the method:
- It is penance without repentance.
- It is justification by works rather than justification by grace.
- It is religion based on what people "do" rather than religion based on what God has "done."

According to John's gospel, some people among the 5000 folks fed by Jesus followed Him the next day. They hoped for another miraculous provision. When it was evident no such miracle was coming, they asked:

> *"What must we do to do the works God requires?"*
> *29 Jesus answered, "The work of God is this: to believe in the one he has sent."* John 6:28b-29 NIV

Again, the question of "doing" what God requires is raised. Jesus reveals a righteous standing with the Lord comes by faith/belief in God's son, not through religious activities.

God's Reply

> *8 He has shown you, O mortal, what is good.*
> *And what does the Lord require of you?*
> *To act justly and to love mercy*
> *and to walk humbly with your God.* Micah 6:8 NIV

This is the best-known verse in the book of Micah. A copy of this verse hangs on the wall of my study. It is a simple and sound description of a quality relationship with the Lord.

What is good? What is required? It was not religious ceremonies and extravagant sacrifices. Instead, a humble walk with the Lord is necessary. This verse was recently the theme of our Student Ministry's *DiscipleNow Weekend*. Jake Spratlin, our church's Minister of Students, shared the wisdom of considering this verse backwards: If we walk humbly with our God, the result will be acting justly and loving mercy.

Walking humbly with God requires a heart of penance and repentance. The only people God can save are lost people who confess they are lost. And the only people God can forgive are guilty people who know they are guilty.

ISRAEL'S IMPENDING JUDGMENT

> *9 Listen! The Lord is calling to the city—*
> *and to fear your name is wisdom—*
> *"Heed the rod and the One who appointed it.* Micah 6:9 NIV

Again Micah calls upon his audience to *Listen*. This time, however, it is not the mountains who should listen but the people. His counsel echoes the theme of the book of Proverbs: *The fear of the Lord is the Beginning of wisdom* (Proverbs 1:7). Sometimes, a good dose of fear inspires us to "heed" to righteous ways.

Their Wrongs

Micah followed by giving two examples of their wickedness.

- **Dishonest Business**

    > *10 Am I still to forget your ill-gotten treasures, you wicked house,*
    > *and the short ephah, which is accursed?*
    > *11 Shall I acquit someone with dishonest scales,*
    > *with a bag of false weights?* Micah 6:10-11 NIV

An *ephah* was a unit of dry measurement equivalent to a bushel. Micah condemns the practices of selling goods that appear full but were actually "short" of a complete *ephah*. I do not go to the grocery store often. Still, I notice that 12-ounce bags of coffee look like they could contain a full pound. Ice cream that once was sold in one-half gallon containers now contain 1.5 quarts. We call that "shrinkflation." Imagine how deceived we would be without laws requiring truth in labeling. It would be the same if dishonest weights or scales were as common in our day as in Micah's time.

- **Violence**

    12 Your rich people are violent;
    your inhabitants are liars
    and their tongues speak deceitfully. Micah 6:12 NIV

    Our previous lesson described violence of tearing off flesh and breaking bones (Micah 3:2-3). The rich gained their wealth on the backs of the poor. The Mosaic economic system provided for the care of the poor and the needy. But the wealthy merchants robbed the poor of both justice and life's necessities. Remember Micah telling how the rich lay in their beds thinking of schemes for acquiring more lands (Micah 2:1-2). It was like Robin Hood in reverse: The rich stealing from the poor.

Their Consequences

13 Therefore, I have begun to destroy you,
to ruin you because of your sins.

Their corruption would not escape punishment. Notice their downfall takes place in two very different stages.

- **Slowly But Surely**

    Despite their plans and the appearance of progress, their efforts would come up empty.

14 You will eat but not be satisfied;
    your stomach will still be empty.
You will store up but save nothing,
    because what you save I will give to the sword.
15 You will plant but not harvest;
    you will press olives but not use the oil,
    you will crush grapes but not drink the wine. Micah 6:14-15 NIV

They thought life was going to be fruitful, productive, and satisfying. While they did not know it, their downfall had begun already. All the things they tried to accumulate would be of no use to them.

Often the worst damage cannot be seen. A person can have serious health issues that conceal any symptoms. An automobile engine may have a major problem that does not call attention to itself. In its earliest stages, a flaw in the foundation of your house is not seen. But the damage is present, real, and growing. The harm of sin often begins in subtle and unseen ways.

- **Suddenly and Openly**

16 You have observed the statutes of Omri
    and all the practices of Ahab's house;
    you have followed their traditions.
Therefore I will give you over to ruin
    and your people to derision;
    you will bear the scorn of the nations Micah 6:16 NIV

Instead of pursuing the Lord, they followed the ways of Kings Omri and Ahab. The book of 1 Kings identifies both rulers as doing "evil in the eyes of the Lord."

> *But Omri did evil in the eyes of the Lord and sinned more than all those before him.* 1 Kings 16:25 NIV
> *Ahab son of Omri did more evil in the eyes of the Lord than any of those before him.* 1 Kings 16:30 NIV

Omri was worse than any before until his son Ahab took the throne. Then Ahab was said to be more evil than even his father. In time, the following of bad examples would bring sudden and open *ruin, derision,* and international *scorn.*

MICAH'S SORROW

Jeremiah is known as *The Weeping Prophet.* But other prophets wept too. These verses express the grief of Micah:

What misery is mine!
I am like one who gathers summer fruit
  at the gleaning of the vineyard;
there is no cluster of grapes to eat,
  none of the early figs that I crave.
2 The faithful have been swept from the land;
  not one upright person remains. Micah 7:1-2a NIV

Micah compared himself to someone looking for good fruit. Alas, there was none. In reality, he was looking for an upright person. Sadly, there were none.

In the next verses Micah condemned sins such as crime and bribery. Afterwards, he elaborated on a deeper issue: the lack of trust.

No One Trusts Anyone

Do not trust a neighbor;
put no confidence in a friend.
Even with the woman who lies in your embrace
guard the words of your lips.
6 For a son dishonors his father,
a daughter rises up against her mother,
a daughter-in-law against her mother-in-law—
a man's enemies are the members of his own household.
Micah 7:5-6 NIV

The lack of trust was so great, neither neighbor, friend, nor family can be trusted. These are the relationships we typically give the MOST trust. Now truth was no longer an expected standard. They assumed everyone is lying. Sadly, when trust disappears, society starts to fall apart.

Jesus quoted this verse in Matthew 10:35-36. Here He taught that He did not come to bring peace, but a sword. His point was that following Him would result in division and contention even within family relationships.

But the Lord Is Trustworthy

But as for me, I watch in hope for the Lord,
I wait for God my Savior;
my God will hear me. Micah 7:7 NIV

Even when no one can be trusted, God's trustworthiness is proclaimed by multiple voices.

- **The Fallen Hebrews**

Do not gloat over me, my enemy!
Though I have fallen, I will rise.
Though I sit in darkness,
the Lord will be my light.
9 Because I have sinned against him,
I will bear the Lord's wrath,
until he pleads my case
and upholds my cause.
He will bring me out into the light;
I will see his righteousness. Micah 7:8-9 NIV

Here was a prophecy of the people's future confession and repentance. They acknowledged *I have fallen.* While circumstances were difficult, there was no cause for gloating and every reason for confidence. Life even at its worse is not without hope. While the Hebrews struggled, they held that a better day was coming when their darkness would be transformed into light. However, a worse day was coming for their gloating enemies:

Then my enemy will see it
and will be covered with shame, Micah 7:10a NIV

- **The Prophet**

The voice of the text returns to Micah speaking optimistically to the people.

The day for building your walls will come,

> *the day for extending your boundaries.*
> *12 In that day people will come to you*
>   *from Assyria and the cities of Egypt,*
> *even from Egypt to the Euphrates*
>   *and from sea to sea*
>   *and from mountain to mountain.* Micah 7:11-12 NIV

Beyond the time of warfare, after walls are destroyed and borders shrink, new walls will be built and boundaries will be expanded. Soon, Assyria and Babylon will arrive with armies. Still, God was orchestrating a day when Palestine would be a destination point for pilgrims from Assyria, Egypt, Babylon and more faraway lands.

- **The Lord**

Finally, the voice of the Lord speaks of what He promises to do.

> *"As in the days when you came out of Egypt,*
>   *I will show them my wonders."*
> *16 Nations will see and be ashamed,*
>   *deprived of all their power.* Micah 7:15-16 NIV

Notice the comparison to the Exodus out of Egypt. It was the most impressive deliverance to date in their history. When the Hebrews came out of Egypt there were many *wonders* such as the ten plagues, a guiding column of fire, a parting sea, and supplies of food. Now God says their deliverance will be equally impressive and full of wonders.

Like other Minor Prophets, Micah was candid about their sins and consequences. But he ends on a high note of mercy and grace.

18 Who is a God like you,
 who pardons sin and forgives the transgression
 of the remnant of his inheritance?
You do not stay angry forever
 but delight to show mercy.
19 You will again have compassion on us;
 you will tread our sins underfoot
 and hurl all our iniquities into the depths of the sea. Micah 7:18-19 NIV

Do you remember what Micah's name meant? Its meaning is the same as the first phrase of verse 18: *Who is like God?* Of course, the answer is *No one!* The Lord is completely trustworthy. His character is to show mercy, express compassion, and forgive sins. The better we know the heart of God, the more we can trust Him with our present life, our future life, and our eternal life.

Paul's letter to Timothy quotes what he calls a "trustworthy saying."

If we are faithless, he remains faithful, 2 Timothy 2:13 NIV

The verdict is in: We are guilty. We are untrustworthy. But we have every reason to trust in God to forgive, care, and restore. Therefore, be spiritual AND religious. It is not an *Either/Or* option. It is *Both.*

A Long Walk with the Minor Prophets

MICAH by Jay McCluskey
Sung to the tune of *My Guy* written by Smokey Robinson
and recorded by Mary Wells.

Nothing you can say
Can change me or my ways, O Micah
Nothing you can do
Will make me hear you. O Micah

We're sticking with our idols and all of our gods
Even against all the odds. They're made out of logs
Were saying right here
You've got nothing we fear, O Micah.

Nothing you can preach
Will be enough to beseech me Micah
Nothing you can sell
Will make me get well, O Micah

We made our promise to a statue named Baal
Bring on the Assyrians, we won't fail
Cause we're from Abram's line
Things will work out just fine, O Micah

Take your Prophecy back to Moresheth
There will be no defeat nor any death.
As a matter of truth you have nothing to flaunt
We like false prophets who say what we want

We'll get riches and fame
There's no wrong to blame, O Micah.
We'll increase our land
Taking down the little man, O Micah.

You can say Do Justice, Love Mercy, Walk with God
But to us that sounds like He's a fraud.

A Long Walk with the Minor Prophets

There's not a sermon you say
That can sway us away, O Micah.

We'll get riches and fame
There's no wrong to blame O Micah.
We'll increase our land
Taking down the little man, O Micah.

You can say Do Justice, Love Mercy, Walk with God
But to us that sounds like He's a fraud.
There's not a sermon you say
That can sway us away, O Micah.

A Long Walk with the Minor Prophets

15 – Nahum
Chapters 1 - 3
Talking About You

Every year, I go away in early October to focus on one of my administrative tasks: writing staff evaluations. When I return, I meet individually with each employee to review his or her job review. Each time I open the conversation by saying the same thing to every staff member: *I did not write TO you. I wrote ABOUT you TO the Church Personnel Committee.*

Nahum did not write TO Nineveh. He wrote ABOUT Nineveh (the Capital of Assyria). He actually wrote TO Judah. By contrast, Jonah preached TO Nineveh. Naman, however, gave his message TO the Hebrews, assuring them that their nemesis, the Assyrian empire, would come to its end.

INTRODUCTION

Not much is known about Nahum except he comes from the town of Elkosh.

A prophecy concerning Nineveh. The book of the vision of Nahum the Elkoshite. Nahum 1:1 NIV

He was the first prophet in our study who ministered entirely after both the fall of Israel in 722 BC and the near defeated Judah in 702 BC (the days of Hezekiah). In Hezekiah's time, Judah was spared when God's intervention caused the Assyrians to withdraw (2 Kings 19).

However, Assyria still loomed large over the tiny kingdom of Judah. The Hebrews questioned whether they were on the wrong side. Assyria seemed like a big bully to tiny Judah. The northern kingdom of Israel was gone. Were they next?

While most prophets were primarily *forthtellers*, Nahum played the prophetic role of *foreteller*. He described the future fall of Nineveh.

Finding the date of Nahum's ministry is aided by a helpful "rule of thumb" I learned in seminary: *A prophet lived after what he references and before what he predicts.*

- Nahum refers to the fall of an Egyptian city named Thebes in 663 BC.

- Nahum predicts the fall of Nineveh which takes place at the hands of the Babylonians in 612 BC.

- Therefore, Nahum can be dated sometime in the early to mid 600s BC

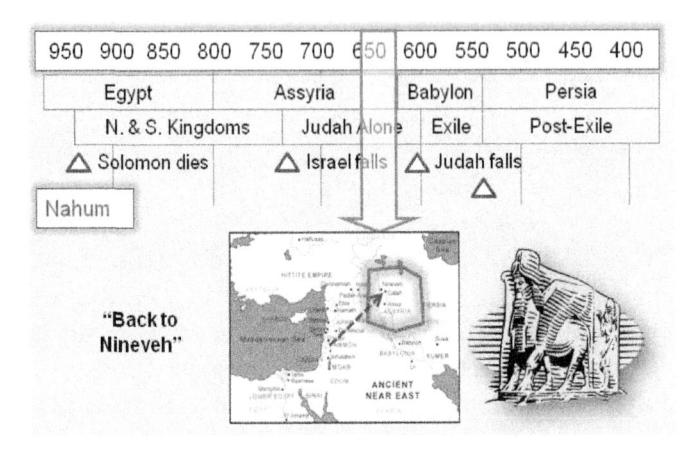

The spirit behind Jonah's message to Nineveh appeared to be a "repent or perish" situation. Nahum's message spoke of Assyria's certain downfall. Each chapter addresses an important question:

- Chapter 1: With whom are you dealing?
- Chapter 2: What is coming your way?
- Chapter 3: Why is this happening?

WITH WHOM ARE YOU DEALING?

Nahum opened his prophecy by reminding his audience of the characteristics of the Lord. Judah may look small when compared to the mass Assyrian Empire. But Assyria is tiny when compared to Judah's great God!

The Lord is a jealous and avenging God;
  the Lord takes vengeance and is filled with wrath.
The Lord takes vengeance on his foes
  and vents his wrath against his enemies.
3 The Lord is slow to anger but great in power;
  the Lord will not leave the guilty unpunished. Nahum 1:2-3

Take a brief look at seven of the Lord's features in this chapter.

Jealous

Jealousy is a sin if it means being envious of something others have and wanting to possess it. However, jealousy is a virtue if it means cherishing what we have and wanting to protect it. God is jealous when the devotion He alone deserves is granted to something else.

Avenging

Vengeance is usually presented as a sin to avoid. But God is rightfully given the responsibility of avenging wrong. He alone knows when and how to apply justice. This characteristic of God is also described in Deuteronomy and Romans:

I will take vengeance on my adversaries and repay those who hate me. Deuteronomy 32:35, 41 NIV

Do not take revenge, my dear friends, but leave room for God's wrath, for it is written: "It is mine to avenge; I will repay," says the Lord. Romans 12:19 NIV

Relegating vengeance to God would be easier if He chose to avenge wrong on **my** timeline and according to **my** preferred ways. Most folks would not mind if occasionally God took up vengeance like John Wayne: standing boldly, immediately, and aggressively against the bad guys in the old westerns. Nahum, however, prescribed patience and trust. God's vengeance will occur in His own time and in His way.

Slow to Anger

The Lord's anger is a holy and righteous indignation. Still, the word "slow" reveals He is not prone to rage or temper tantrums. Remember, one of the *Fruit of the Spirit* is "self-control." Practicing self-control when angry is a most challenging undertaking.

Just

The Lord will not leave the guilty unpunished. Nahum 1:3b NIV

During my college years I learned the *Evangelism Explosion* presentation of the gospel. This method affirms God's justice by utilizing a near identical verse to Nahum's words.

Yet he does not leave the guilty unpunished Exodus 34:7b NIV

In His mercy God allowed a substitute to take our punishment. Jesus' sacrifice on the cross ultimately satisfied the Lord's requirement for justice.

Powerful

The mountains quake before him
  and the hills melt away.
The earth trembles at his presence,
  the world and all who live in it. Nahum 1:5 NIV

One of the worship songs we commonly sing is entitled, *The Great I AM*. The lyrics include a powerful and dramatic phrase which sounds much like the opening line of this verse: *The mountains shake before Him.*

The citizens of Judah wondered if God was absent or weak. Even though God does not *quake*, there is no reason to conclude He is incapable of acting dramatically.

Good

The Lord is good, a refuge in times of trouble.
He cares for those who trust in him, Nahum 1:7a NIV

Here is a solid general statement of God's compassionate care. Nahum went on to specify how Judah can and will experience the Lord's goodness.

Look, there on the mountains,
the feet of one who brings good news,
who proclaims peace!
Celebrate your festivals, Judah,
and fulfill your vows.
No more will the wicked invade you;
they will be completely destroyed. Nahum 1:15 NIV

In ancient times, news was delivered by messengers. Sentries posted on city walls watched for messengers bringing news, preferably good news. Isaiah used this same statement where a messenger shares the defeat of Babylon (Isaiah 52:7). Later, Paul quotes it in Romans, applying it to those who share the gospel (Romans 10:15).

The news ahead is good! You have reason to celebrate.

Sovereign

Whatever they plot against the Lord
he will bring to an end;
trouble will not come a second time.
10 They will be entangled among thorns Nahum 1:9-10a NIV

As stated in the introduction to this study, in 702 BC the Assyrian army marched to the walls of Jerusalem. Nineveh's military had plans to invade and take Judah's capital. But after God intervened, they had to retreat to Assyria (2 Kings 18-19). While the

Assyrians had plans, God's plans ultimately prevailed. I like this simple adage affirming God's sovereignty: *If you want to make God laugh, tell him your plans!*

WHAT IS COMING YOUR WAY?

Having affirmed the powerful nature of the Lord, Nahum addressed the future fall of Assyria. While Assyria appeared formidable, tough times were ahead.

The Invasion Is Coming

An attacker advances against you, Nineveh.
  Guard the fortress,
  watch the road,
  brace yourselves,
  marshal all your strength! Nahum 2:1 NIV

Notice the words describing the Assyrian military on defense: guarding, watching, and digging in. In contrast, an impressive army on the offensive was advancing toward them.

The shields of the soldiers are red;
  the warriors are clad in scarlet.
The metal on the chariots flashes
  on the day they are made ready;
  the spears of juniper are brandished. Nahum 2:3 NIV

The City Is Falling

The river gates are thrown open
  and the palace collapses. Nahum 2:6 NIV

The Khoser River flowed through Nineveh. Historians tell how Nineveh's invaders dammed up the river then suddenly released its flow. The rush of water flooded the city, destroying part of the wall and some of the buildings. Nahum described this outcome a couple of verses later.

Nineveh is like a pool
 whose water is draining away. Nahum 2:8a NIV

The Ninevites Are Mocked

Nahum contrasted Nineveh's present glory with their future embarrassment.

Where now is the lions' den,
 the place where they fed their young,
where the lion and lioness went,
 and the cubs, with nothing to fear? Nahum 2:11 NIV

The image of the lion often was used by the Assyrians in their art and architecture. This image was meant to communicate strength and fierceness. Here, *the lions* are absent.

Later in Chapter 3, Nahum further described Nineveh's coming humiliation.

"I am against you," declares the Lord Almighty.
 "I will lift your skirts over your face.
I will show the nations your nakedness
 and the kingdoms your shame.
6 I will pelt you with filth,
 I will treat you with contempt
 and make you a spectacle. Nahum 3:5-6 NIV

Lifting a person's *skirts* or robe resulted in their shame! The word *filth* translates *detestable* or *abominable* things. Being targeted with *filth* brought deep disgrace.

R.G. Lee was a noted Baptist preacher in the early 1900's. His signature sermon was *Payday Someday*. Nahum voiced God's declaration to Nineveh: *Your payday is coming!*

"I am against you,"
 declares the Lord Almighty.
"I will burn up your chariots in smoke,
 and the sword will devour your young lions.
I will leave you no prey on the earth.
The voices of your messengers
 will no longer be heard." Nahum 2:13 NIV

WHAT DID YOU DO?

Chapter 3 turns the topic to Nahum's final question: What did you do to cause this to occur?

Ruthlessness

Nahum described their cruelty and bloodshed.

Woe to the city of blood,
 full of lies,
full of plunder,
 never without victims! Nahum 3:1 NIV
Many casualties,
 piles of dead,
bodies without number,
 people stumbling over the corpses— Nahum 3:3b NIV

The Assyrians stacked up corpses of their enemies like firewood. This image served as a warning to anyone who would oppose them. Death is always unpleasant. But this degree of Assyrian malice was totally senseless.

Prideful

In Nahum's time, Nineveh seemed impregnable. Still, it would be destroyed. Their false assurance was compared to the Egyptian city of Thebes.

Are you better than Thebes,
  situated on the Nile,
with water around her?
The river was her defense,
  the waters her wall.
9 Cush and Egypt were her boundless strength;
  Put and Libya were among her allies.
10 Yet she was taken captive
  and went into exile.
Her infants were dashed to pieces
  at every street corner.
Lots were cast for her nobles,
  and all her great men were put in chains. Nahum 3:8-10 NIV

Thebes was the capital city of Upper Egypt. Its location and fortifications were thought to ensure its safety from any invader. Despite its position and its allies, the city still fell to defeat. Nineveh would fare no better.

All your fortresses are like fig trees
  with their first ripe fruit;
when they are shaken,

> *the figs fall into the mouth of the eater.* Nahum 3:12 NIV

Certain fruit, when ripe, falls very easily from the tree. One day, the time would be "ripe" for Nineveh's downfall. Only a small *shake* was necessary for Nineveh to drop into the "mouth" of its adversary.

CONCLUSION – YOUR DOOM IS SURE

In Martin Luther's hymn *A Mighty Fortress Is Our God* a verse says of Satan:

Lo his doom is sure. One little word will fell Him.

Like other prophets in our study, Nahum used similes to describe Nineveh and her impending doom. To Nahum, Nineveh was like victims of a locust invasion and sleeping shepherds.

Devouring and Disappearing Locust

The sword bringing about Nineveh's ruin would devour them like a swarm of locusts.

> *There the fire will consume you;*
> *the sword will cut you down—*
> *they will devour you like a swarm of locusts.* Nahum 3:15 NIV

There was "poetic justice" in this fate. The greed and aggression of Assyrian merchants themselves had "stripped the land" like locusts.

> *You have increased the number of your merchants*
> *till they are more numerous than the stars in the sky,*

> *but like locusts they strip the land
>   and then fly away.* Nahum 3:16 NIV

Notice the locusts fly away. A locust plague is catastrophic. But their ongoing presence is not sustainable. Eventually they die out or disappear. In time, the fierce damage comes to an end. So it was with Nineveh. The saying declares *All good things must come to an end.* But Nahum assured the Hebrews their difficult struggles with the Assyrians would too come to an end.

Slumbering Shepherds

> *King of Assyria, your shepherds slumber;
>   your nobles lie down to rest.
> Your people are scattered on the mountains
>   with no one to gather them.* Nahum 3:18 NIV

When shepherds are negligent, the sheep scatter. Remember Micah's condemnation of Hebrew leaders. They were part of the community's problems rather than a source of solutions. The role of "nobles" is to be alert and attentive to others. Instead, Nineveh's leaders slept on the job.

Fatally Wounded

> *Nothing can heal you;
>   your wound is fatal.* Nahum 3:19a

Again, God's message to Nineveh during Jonah's prophecy was "repent or perish." Fortunately, they chose to repent. In contrast, no such hope was granted in Nahum's prophecy to that same city.

Their doom was sure. No healing would arrive. Their demise was just a matter of time.

Amid hardship, difficulty, and persecution, God's people may well feel like they are on the wrong side. But Nahum affirmed the game was not over. The final score was not yet posted. God was powerful, wise, and true. Therefore, be faithful. The Lord will prevail in the end.

In the flow of history, nations and empires rise and fall. But Father Time is undefeated. Even the physically strong eventually become weak. Folks can hang from a bar with a tight grip. But gravity prevails. As a precaution, I recently took a cardiac stress test where I walked on a speedy treadmill. Just after my college years, I worked in the Heart Center of a hospital. Therefore, I knew a fundamental fact about this exam: *The treadmill always wins. It is just a matter of time.* Likewise, we can be confident of God's ultimate victory.

Oppression and disappointment may reside for a while. Still, Nahum the *minor* prophet left us with a *major* truth: **The awfulness of man is no match for the awesomeness of our God.**

BAD BAD NINEVEH

Sung to the of *Bad Bad Leroy Brown* written and recorded by Jim Croce.

On the north side of Mesopotamia
Where empires come and go.
And in Nahum's time
The place doing crime
Was the city of Nineveh.

Now Nineveh was a "lion."
She was cruel and full of pride
But Nahum cried,
"You're not on God's side.
Your end will come.
Your cause has died.

You're Bad, Bad, Nineveh
Capital of Assyria
Once badder than a locust swarm
You're gonna go down to God's reform.

The Lord said, "I'm a just God.
Slow to anger and jealous too.
You're on the ropes
You attacked my folks
I'm sovereign so you'll be through.

Oh Nineveh, I'm against you.
You'll be disgraced and full of shame.
You'll be a spectacle, disrespectable,
An embarrassment to your name.

You're Bad, Bad, Nineveh
Capital of Assyria
Once badder than a locust swarm

A Long Walk with the Minor Prophets

You're gonna go down to God's reform.

You're Bad, Bad, Nineveh
Capital of Assyria
Once badder than a locust swarm
You're gonna go down to God's reform.

16 – ZEPHANIAH
Zephaniah 1 - 3
The Darkness Shall Turn to Dawning

In the study of Jonah, I referred to the hymn *We've a Story to Tell to The Nations*, published by H. Earnest Nichol in 1896. The song's melody moves with a quick march tempo arriving to a confidant refrain declaring, *The Darkness shall turn to the Dawning*. Zephaniah's prophecy starts with a "dark" mood of judgment upon the Hebrews and their neighbors. In the end, the prophecy turns into the bright "dawn" of coming ultimate hope and rescue.

INTRODUCTION

1 The word of the Lord that came to Zephaniah son of Cushi, the son of Gedaliah, the son of Amariah, the son of Hezekiah, during the reign of Josiah son of Amon king of Judah: Zephaniah 1:1 NIV

While Nahum's introduction reveals only his hometown, the single verse about Zephaniah gives us several bits of

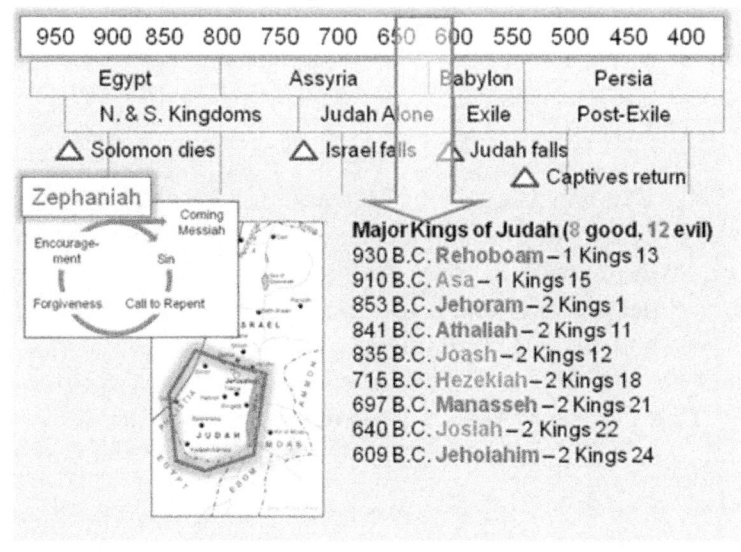

950	900	850	800	750	700	650	600	550	500	450	400
Egypt				Assyria			Babylon			Persia		
N. & S. Kingdoms			Judah Alone		Exile		Post-Exile		
△ Solomon dies			△ Israel falls		△ Judah falls			
								△ Captives return		

Major Kings of Judah (8 good, 12 evil)
930 B.C. Rehoboam – 1 Kings 13
910 B.C. Asa – 1 Kings 15
853 B.C. Jehoram – 2 Kings 1
841 B.C. Athaliah – 2 Kings 11
835 B.C. Joash – 2 Kings 12
715 B.C. Hezekiah – 2 Kings 18
697 B.C. Manasseh – 2 Kings 21
640 B.C. Josiah – 2 Kings 22
609 B.C. Jehoiahim – 2 Kings 24

information. For example, his name means *Jehovah protects*. And if the Hezekiah named in his linage is the same as King Hezekiah of Judah (715-686), then the prophet Zephaniah was this king's great-great-grandson. If Zephaniah had "royal" blood. Perhaps he was related to King Josiah who reigned during Zephaniah's ministry (640-609 BC). Josiah's time is remembered for his reforms. However, Zephaniah's judgmental tone suggests he prophesized prior to Josiah's transformations.

GOD'S MASSIVE JUDGMENT

Chapter 1 mentions *The Day of the Lord* five times (vv, 7, 8, 14, 18). This term identifies a future time when God rewards those living in faithfulness and rebukes the unfaithful. Some *Day of the Lord* references are to the end times and some occur beforehand.

The Extent of God's Judgment

*"I will sweep away everything
from the face of the earth,"*
declares the Lord.
3 *"I will sweep away both man and beast;* Zephaniah 1:2-3a NIV

The word *sweep* can be translated *consume* or *remove*. The included ruin of even the animals reminds me of the story of Noah and the flood's destruction of people and creatures. God does not do any task halfway, even judgment.

The Cause of God's Judgment

As in many generations before, the Hebrews rebelled against the Lord through the worship of false gods and idols.

I will destroy every remnant of Baal worship in this place,
    the very names of the idolatrous priests—
those who bow down on the roofs
    to worship the starry host,
those who bow down and swear by the Lord
    and who also swear by Molek, Zephaniah 1:4b-5 NIV

Baal was the god of fertility appealed to for fruitfulness. Molek was a Canaanite god often noted as the recipient of child sacrifices. These verses identify violation of both the First Commandment (have no other gods before the Lord) and the Second Commandment (create no graven images).

Sad Responses to God's Judgment

those who turn back from following the Lord
    and neither seek the Lord nor inquire of him." Zephaniah 1:6 NIV

Here is a troubling summary of the Hebrew people. While the Bible has many inspiring verses, this is a sad verse. Their spiritual life was in retreat at worst or in neutral at best. Such unfaithfulness results in several disappointing responses to God's judgment.

- **Silence**

Be silent before the Sovereign Lord,
    for the day of the Lord is near. Zephaniah 1:7a NIV

People placed under arrest are reminded of their "right to remain silent." The idea is that saying anything would only give opportunity for their words to be used to prove their guilt. When people are confronted about their wrongs, silence is often an instinctive response. In the presence of *the Sovereign Lord* silence is appropriate. There are no words to say.

- **Sacrifice**

The description here is unique in that God makes the sacrifice! The reference to *the Lord's sacrifice* is followed with a description of punishment He issues.

"On the day of the Lord's sacrifice
I will punish the officials
and the king's sons
and all those clad
in foreign clothes. Zephaniah 1:8 NIV

A sacrificial price must be paid for sin. The people who follow the Lord understand a substitute sacrifice is available. Here, God carries out the sacrifice as the wages of sin on the leadership and the wealthy. Therefore, God's justice is served.

Notice the phrase "*all those clad in foreign clothes.* After preparing this study, I checked out the tags on many of my clothing items. My suspicions were confirmed: most of my garments were manufactured in foreign lands. For us, this is common. But in Biblical days, clothes imported from distant lands were only affordable to the wealthy.

- **Wailing**

    "On that day,"
    declares the Lord,
    "a cry will go up from the Fish Gate,
    wailing from the New Quarter,
    and a loud crash from the hills. Zephaniah 1:10 NIV

    Zephaniah clearly had working knowledge of the layout of Jerusalem. As a result of God's judgment, the intensity of their *wails* will be loud and extensive.

    Today, the ancient western wall of Herod's Temple is called "The Wailing Wall." Orthodox Hebrews in Jerusalem go to this place to practice their spiritual exercise of "wailing" or crying out to God. Observers will note the stones making up the women's side of the Wailing Wall are darker in tone. A tour guide explained how this coloring was the result of all the ladies' tears that fell upon the wall.

- **Complacency**

    At that time I will search Jerusalem with lamps
    and punish those who are complacent,
    who are like wine left on its dregs,
    who think, 'The Lord will do nothing,
    either good or bad.' Zephaniah 1:12 NIV

When a town is defeated, the victorious army must search for people hiding. Usually, the people taking cover are the militant ones who refuse to surrender. But here the search is for the *complacent*. I found five English versions translating this expression as *stagnant in spirit*. They are like unstirred wine that congeals and develops bitter dregs.

Their cry testifies of their stagnation: *The Lord will do nothing*. In their bland complacency, they could not even imagine the fall of God's judgment upon them.

- **Helplessness**

Neither their silver nor their gold
  will be able to save them
  on the day of the Lord's wrath." Zephaniah 1:18

Relying on *silver* and *gold* to save themselves was useless. Money can buy our way out of some trouble and pains. But there are problems that no amount of wealth can fix. I heard this week of a skilled and successful surgeon diagnosed with a rare disease. Even with every medical resource available, he did not defeat his illness. Likewise, worldly wealth cannot buy our way out of the judgment of God.

Better Responses to God's Judgment

Turning to chapter 2, Zephaniah offers better responses in anticipation of the coming Day of the Lord.

- **Assemble**

*Gather together, gather yourselves together,
    you shameful nation,
2 before the decree takes effect
    and that day passes like windblown chaff,* Zephaniah 2:1-2a NIV

Zephaniah calls the nation to a "solemn assembly." It was a time of confession and repentance. Such a gathering did occur in Zephaniah's lifetime as Josiah responded to the discovery of the book of the law and the instructions of the prophetess Huldah (2 Chronicles 34:29-31).

- **Seek**

*Seek the Lord, all you humble of the land,
    you who do what he commands.
Seek righteousness, seek humility;
    perhaps you will be sheltered
    on the day of the Lord's anger.* Zephaniah 2:3 NIV

Rather than seek after idols and pagan ways, Zephaniah called the people to pursue three noble directions: seek the Lord, seek righteousness, and seek humility.

A hint of hope for avoiding God's judgment is in the phrase, *perhaps you will be sheltered on the day of the Lord's anger*. Zephaniah is preaching the possibility that the meaning of his name will be fulfilled: *The Lord Protects*. Maybe there was a chance! When Jonah declared the destruction of Nineveh, the king called for fasting and repentance saying, *God may yet relent and with compassion turn from his fierce anger so that we will not perish* (Jonah 3:9 NIV). God responded to their repentance with mercy. Perhaps He would show mercy to the Hebrews if they repented.

Soon, under Josiah's reign, the Hebrews recognized their sin, repented, and experienced good reforms. Unfortunately, when Josiah died in battle, the following four kings returned to their rebellious way.

JUDGMENT ROLL CALL OF THE NATIONS

Amos prophesied against other nations before eventually speaking out against the Hebrews. Zephaniah takes an opposite approach, turning his words against surrounding nations AFTER prophesying against the Hebrews.

The four directions of the compass are represented in the four nations singled out. While Zephaniah does not give specific details of their rebellion, he gave a "bottom line" declaration of their approaching destruction.

Philistia – (West)

Gaza will be abandoned
  and Ashkelon left in ruins. Zephaniah 2:4a NIV

the word of the Lord is against you,
  Canaan, land of the Philistines.
He says, "I will destroy you,
  and none will be left." Zechariah 2:5b NIV

That land will belong

> *to the remnant of the people of Judah;* Zephaniah 2:7a NIV

Nebuchadnezzar attacked Philistia and destroyed it in 604 BC. The only remnant of it today is the word *Palestine* which comes from the word *Philistine*.

Moab and Ammon (East)

> *"I have heard the insults of Moab*
> *and the taunts of the Ammonites,*
> *who insulted my people*
> *and made threats against their land.*
> *9 Therefore, as surely as I live,"*
> *declares the Lord Almighty,*
> *the God of Israel,*
> *"surely Moab will become like Sodom,*
> *the Ammonites like Gomorrah—* Zephaniah 2:8-9 NIV

The Moabites and the Ammonites were descendants of Lot. In Genesis, Lot is associated with the story of Sodom and Gomorrah's destruction (Genesis 19). Thus, this comparison is fitting.

Cush (South)

> *"You Cushites, too,*
> *will be slain by my sword."* Zephaniah 2:12 NIV

The Cushite people resided in the upper Nile region. In 590 BC their capital, Napata, was sacked by the Egyptian pharaoh Psammeticus II. According to Zephaniah, their fall was imminent.

Assyria (North)

This is the city of revelry
 that lived in safety.
She said to herself,
 "I am the one! And there is none besides me."
What a ruin she has become,
 a lair for wild beasts!
All who pass by her scoff
 and shake their fists. Zephaniah 2:15 NIV

Do you remember our previous study of Nahum's condemnation of Nineveh, Assyria's capital? At the end of the seventh century, the Assyrian empire collapsed under the assault of the Babylonians. As a result, Assyria was no longer the dominate empire it was before.

Jerusalem

In chapter 3, the prophet's attention returns to Jerusalem. Even the city which was home to the Lord's temple would not escape God's judgment.

She does not trust in the Lord,
 she does not draw near to her God. Zephaniah 3:2c NIV

This is a general description of their spiritual condition. The following verses present five specific examples of their failure to trust.

- **No Obedience**

She obeys no one, Zephaniah 3:2a NIV

The root of sin is our demand to control our own life. Judah refused to answer to God's will and way.

- **No Instruction**

    she accepts no correction. Zephaniah 3:2b NIV

    Proverbs 15:32 states, *Those who disregard discipline despise themselves, but the one who heeds correction gains understanding.* Judah foolishly rejected God's efforts to correct their direction.

- **No Leadership**

    *Her officials within her
       are roaring lions;
    her rulers are evening wolves,
       who leave nothing for the morning.
    4 Her prophets are unprincipled;
       they are treacherous people.
    Her priests profane the sanctuary
       and do violence to the law.* Zephaniah 3:3-4 NIV

    Like previous prophets, Zephaniah spotlights the corruption of the leaders. Their dishonesty was widespread and across the board. This dynamic included *prophets, priests, and kings (officials)*.

- **No Shame**

    *The Lord within her is righteous;
       he does no wrong.
    Morning by morning he dispenses his justice,
       and every new day he does not fail,
       yet the unrighteous know no shame.* Zephaniah 3:5 NIV

Zephaniah presented a simple contrast: God was righteous and faithful while they were unrighteous and shameless. At the dedication of the temple, King Solomon prayed the people's sins would be followed with confession and repentance (1 Kings 8:46-49). But to this generation there was no shame accompanying their misdeeds.

- **No Change**

God expected His people to accept change and correction. Alas, the people, thought otherwise.

Of Jerusalem I thought,
  'Surely you will fear me
  and accept correction!'
Then her place of refuge would not be destroyed,
  nor all my punishments come upon her.
But they were still eager
  to act corruptly in all they did. Zephaniah 3:7

Repentance is more than admitting our sins or even feeling emotional regret for our mistakes. At the heart of repentance is the response Judah lacked: Change.

RESCUE OF THE REMNANT

As our study turns to chapter 3, Zephaniah's declarations move from the dark destiny of the guilty to the light of hope for the faithful. This is a trend we noted in earlier studies of the minor prophets. Ending with words of hope encouraged the faithful through difficult times. This approach also motivated the remnant to act in obedience and stand with the Lord.

I will rescue the lame;
   I will gather the exiles.
I will give them praise and honor
   in every land where they have suffered shame. Zephaniah 3:19b NIV

What is involved in this *rescue?*

Purification

> *"Then I will purify the lips of the peoples,*
>   *that all of them may call on the name of the Lord*
>   *and serve him shoulder to shoulder.* Zephaniah 3:9 NIV

Let us start with the end of this verse. It is so sad when families, friends, church members, communities, and countries turn on each other. In contrast, the prophet sees God uniting His people *shoulder to shoulder.* I earnestly believe the church is called to demonstrate this unity. When God's people hold a common love for Jesus, people of all kinds of cultures and opinions can practice the grace necessary to get along.

They will do no wrong;
   they will tell no lies.
A deceitful tongue
   will not be found in their mouths. Zephaniah 3:13a NIV

The words coming out of them represented the sin living inside of them. God promises to purify the sin of their speech. When Isaiah saw the Lord, he declared himself to be a man of "unclean lips." Purification came when a seraphim took a hot coal and touched it to his lips and mouth (Isaiah 6:5-7).

Words have power. When words fail to serve God's kingdom, His mercy extends forgiveness.

Gathering

From beyond the rivers of Cush
  my worshipers, my scattered people,
  will bring me offerings. Zephaniah 3:10 NIV

Persecution has a way of scattering people. In time, the fall of Jerusalem to Babylon would scatter many of the Hebrews. But a time of great gathering will come forth even from people who lived deep in Africa (Cush). Together these pilgrims will bring their offerings to the Lord.

In recent years, some churches have stopped including a formal offering in their worship time. This change is motivated by a concern for hygiene in "passing the plates" and the growing use of electronic giving. Personally, I still like to *pass the plates.* Giving our offerings is a part of our worship. As in Zephaniah's description, the offering is an action the people of God should practice when gathering.

Humility

I will remove from you
  your arrogant boasters.
Never again will you be haughty
  on my holy hill.
12 But I will leave within you
  the meek and humble. Zephaniah 3:11b-12a NIV

Arrogance and haughty spirits are rejected. But God's work is receptive to meek and humble hearts.

Let the one who boasts boast in the Lord." 1 Corinthians 1:31, Jeremiah 9:24 ESV
God opposes the proud but shows favor to the humble. James 4:6 NIV

Worship

- **The People Rejoice**

Zephaniah refers to God's people with the endearing term *Daughter*.

Sing, Daughter Zion;
shout aloud, Israel!
Be glad and rejoice with all your heart,
Daughter Jerusalem!
15 The Lord has taken away your punishment,
he has turned back your enemy. Zephaniah 3:14-15a NIV

Often in the Bible, God's people respond to his victories by rejoicing in song.

- **The Lord Sings**

He will take great delight in you;
in his love he will no longer rebuke you,
but will rejoice over you with singing. Zephaniah 3:17a NIV

Here is an amazing thought: Our God is a singing God! While we sing praises to our Lord, He rejoices in song over us!

Restoration

Notice the use of the first-person pronoun *I*. The restoration of God's people is His work alone.

At that time I will gather you;
  at that time I will bring you home.
I will give you honor and praise
  among all the peoples of the earth
when I restore your fortunes
  before your very eyes,"
says the Lord. Zephaniah 3:20 NIV

I will bring you home. What a great statement! I love to travel. But inevitably, a journey reaches a point when I am ready to return home.

For Zephaniah's generation, *The Day of the Lord* is literally near. Jerusalem fell to the Babylonians in 587 BC. Afterwards, seventy years of exile occurred. But a promised homecoming and restoration was to follow. Historically, that is an amazing promise. Typically, citizens who were defeated and exiled never returned to their homeland.

In summary: *The Day of the Lord* was coming when God would…

Send Tribulation,
Judge the Nations,
Save His people, and then
Establish His righteous kingdom.

Judgment is coming. Difficulties are coming. It may be tempting to give up or give in. Instead, Zephaniah gave this appeal: Be faithful. Be humble. Be repentant. Rescue and restoration is coming for the remnant of the Lord! His own name gave the assurance: *Zephaniah: The Lord Protects.*

In a rainstorm an umbrella only protects those people who stand under its shelter. Trust in the Lord and in His protection. For the faithful, it will end well:

> *For the darkness WILL turn to the dawning.*
> *And the dawning to noonday bright,*
> *and Christ's great kingdom shall come on earth,*
> *the kingdom of love and light.* - H. Earnest Nichol

ZEPHANIAH by Jay McCluskey
Sung to the tune of *Sweet Caroline* written and recorded by Neal Diamond.

Where it began,
Not in Ammon or Moab
Not in Assyria or Cush.
Complacent hearts
Quick to bow down to idols
For you to fall just takes a push.

Day of the Lord
Sweeping out, sweeping thee, sweeping you!

Zephaniah (God Protects)
You show darkness in our way (Our Way!)
You've been inclined (So Inclined)
To say hope will come some day
But now we're...

Wailing and still
No shame or Godly leaders
Just stubbornness and yet no change.
But when it ends
Purity and our worship
Our restoration will engage.

Trust, in the Lord
Reachin' out, touchin' thee, touchin' you

Zephaniah (God Protects)
You show darkness in our way (Our Way!)
You've been inclined (so inclined)
To say hope will come some day
Oh, say, say

Zephaniah (God Protects)
You show darkness in our way (Our Way!)
You've been inclined (so inclined)
To say hope will come some day
Zephaniah

A Long Walk with the Minor Prophets

17 – HABAKKUK
Habakkuk 1-3
Have A Little Talk with Jehovah

Surprisingly, there are very few extended "back and forth" conversations in the Bible between God and individual people. (If you do not count the conversations of Jesus recorded in the gospels). Here are a few rare examples:
- The story of Moses talking to God at the Burning Bush covers two chapters (Exodus 3-4).
- During Isaiah's calling, his conversation with God takes one chapter (Isaiah 6).
- The prophecy of Habakkuk begins with two chapters of dialogue between Habakkuk and the Lord (Habakkuk 1-2).

Habakkuk's conversation with the Lord inspired the title of this lesson: *Have a little talk with Jehovah*. The gospel song *Have a Little Talk with Jesus* comes from a New Testament perspective. *Jehovah* is a version of the Lord's Hebrew name in the Old Testament: *Yahweh*.

Habakkuk's third chapter is a poem of devotion and praise.

INTRODUCTION

Habakkuk's reference to the rise and advance of the Chaldeans (Habakkuk 1:6–11) dates him in the middle to last quarter of the 7th century BC. It is likely that it was written shortly after the Fall of Nineveh (in 612 BC) and before the Babylonian capture of Jerusalem (in 587 BC). Therefore, his ministry overlapped with Jeremiah and Zephaniah.

The name Habakkuk means "embrace" or "wrestle." Although his name does not appear in any other part of the Jewish Bible, an old Rabbinic tradition holds Habakkuk to be the Shunammite woman's son who was restored to life by Elisha in 2 Kings 4:16.

Our study of the first two chapters will outline the conversation between Habakkuk and the Lord.

LORD, YOU CONFUSE ME

We could say Habakkuk accused God of *infuriating* him. In essence he said, *God! I do not understand what you are doing? … or NOT doing!* Honest believers will confess we occasionally say this to God ourselves!

Lord, you do not seem to listen.

How long, Lord, must I call for help,
  but you do not listen?
Or cry out to you, "Violence!"
  but you do not save? Habakkuk 1:2 NIV

Notice the verbs *call* and *cry*. *Call* means to call for help. *Cry* means to scream with a loud voice. A cry is a call with intensity, urgency, and even anger. Habakkuk felt ignored by God. His patience was wearing thin. Here is an important distinction: <u>An unanswered prayer is not an unheard prayer</u>. Unanswered prayers can feel as if they are unheard. Still, God is all-knowing and aware of all we ask of Him.

Lord, You do not seem concerned about justice.

Why do you make me look at injustice?
  Why do you tolerate wrongdoing?
Destruction and violence are before me;

there is strife, and conflict abounds. Habakkuk 1:3

God declared Himself to be a God of justice. And God's people were themselves to be agents of justice:

> *6 "Do not deny justice to your poor people in their lawsuits. 7 Have nothing to do with a false charge and do not put an innocent or honest person to death, for I will not acquit the guilty.* Exodus 23:6-7 NIV

From Habakkuk's perspective, the wicked were flourishing. There was no justice! It appeared God was allowing what He Himself condemned.

Habakkuk voiced common complaints about God. Feeling ignored and witnessing strife, he wrestled with his doubts about God and His ways. But rather than running away from God, he showed faith by leaning INTO God. In accordance with his name, Habakkuk "embraced" the Lord rather than his doubts and responded to God's reply.

SERVANT, MY WAYS ARE NOT YOUR WAYS

Look at the nations and watch—
and be utterly amazed. Habakkuk 1:5a NIV

Though Habakkuk could not see it, God was at work among the nations. With this response God essentially said, *Habakkuk, You ain't seen nothing yet!*

For I am going to do something in your days
that you would not believe,
even if you were told.
6 I am raising up the Babylonians,
that ruthless and impetuous people,

*who sweep across the whole earth
to seize dwellings not their own.* Habakkuk 1:5-6 NIV

With this word, the prophet was shocked: God was going to punish the Hebrews by using.... the Babylonians! Of all things! The Babylonians would be the tool through which God was going to exercise discipline on the Hebrews. No wonder Habakkuk replied in amazement:

LORD, HOW CAN A WICKED NATION BE USED TO PUNISH YOUR OWN PEOPLE?

*Lord, are you not from everlasting?
My God, my Holy One, you will never die.
You, Lord, have appointed them to execute judgment;
you, my Rock, have ordained them to punish.*

The emotion of this statement translates better if we read the word *them* with lots of emphasis: *You have appointed THEM to execute judgment!* Habakkuk is processing this news that God was preparing the Babylonians to execute His judgment. He questions: *How can a holy God use wicked people?*

*13 Your eyes are too pure to look on evil;
you cannot tolerate wrongdoing.
Why then do you tolerate the treacherous?
Why are you silent while the wicked
swallow up those more righteous than themselves?* Habakkuk 1:12-13 NIV

Habakkuk's question is valid: Why would God let people with "some" righteousness be defeated by people with even 'less" righteousness? Look at how ruthless they are:

The wicked foe pulls all of them up with hooks,

> *he catches them in his net,*
> *he gathers them up in his dragnet;*
> *and so he rejoices and is glad.* Habakkuk 1:15 NIV

How can it reason that the Lord would allow such spiritually ignorant people to conquer His own people? But just because we do not understand why something occurs does not mean God does not have a reason that is beyond our comprehension. Isaiah affirmed: *As the heavens are higher than the earth, so are my ways higher than your ways and my thoughts than your thoughts.* Isaiah 55:9 NIV

LORD, I WILL WAIT FOR YOU

In patient faith, Habakkuk agreed to wait for God's answer:

> *I will stand at my watch*
> *and station myself on the ramparts;*
> *I will look to see what he will say to me,*
> *and what answer I am to give to this complaint.* Habakkuk 2:1 NIV

The prophet saw himself as a guard awaiting the delivery of a divine message to give to the people.

SERVANT, I KNOW WHAT I AM DOING

Turning now to Chapter 2, Habakkuk received God's response to his challenge, assuring the prophet He knew what He was doing.

> *Then the Lord replied:*
> *"Write down the revelation*
> *and make it plain on tablets*
> *so that a herald may run with it.* Habakkuk 2:2 NIV

Here are two quick commands: *Write this down and make it plain!* The fact is, we would not be studying Habakkuk's book if he had not obeyed these instructions. This admonition remains applicable for people sharing God's message today. Written words endure longer than spoken words. Plain words communicate more effectively than complex statements. In follow-up, the Lord gave Habakkuk some practical words of counsel:

The Time Will Come

For the revelation awaits an appointed time;
it speaks of the end
and will not prove false. Habakkuk 2:3a NIV

My son's dog, Theo, is a Golden Doodle. He is trained to respond to numerous instructions, including the command to "stay." Here, God said the same thing said to Habakkuk: *Wait for it...Wait for it....* The revelation of God's answer possessed an appointed arrival time. It could take a while before delivery, but it would come.

Be Assured by What You Can Know

I often affirm *You don't know what you don't know!* This reality will always be true on this side of eternity. Still, there ARE some things you can know. God gave Habakkuk three assurances to embrace:

- **Have faith in God's faithfulness**

    "See, the enemy is puffed up;
    his desires are not upright—

but the righteous person will live by his faithfulness
Habakkuk 2:4 NIV

The phrase, *the righteous person will live by his faithfulness,* is Habakkuk's best-known expression. In the New Testament this statement is quoted in Romans 1:17, Galatians 3:11, and Hebrews 10:38. Each time it affirms how salvation is by faith through God's grace and not by our righteous works.

- **God is just**

God declares 5 *"Woes"* regarding the fate of the people who do evil. Notice the different categories of sins that justly result in "woe."

*"'Woe to him who piles up stolen goods
 and makes himself wealthy by extortion!* Habakkuk 2:6b NIV (stealing)

*"Woe to him who builds his house by unjust gain,
 setting his nest on high
 to escape the clutches of ruin!* Habakkuk 2:9 NIV (corruption)

*"Woe to him who builds a city with bloodshed
 and establishes a town by injustice!* Habakkuk 2:12 NIV (violence)

*"Woe to him who gives drink to his neighbors,
 pouring it from the wineskin till they are drunk,* Habakkuk 2:15a NIV (drunkenness)

Woe to him who says to wood, 'Come to life!'

Or to lifeless stone, 'Wake up!' Habakkuk 2:19a NIV (idolatry)

Here is the conclusion God declared to Habakkuk: Just because something is an instrument of God does not mean He accepts everything it does. I know this is true from personal experience. God certainly does not approve of everything in my life. But I believe He still uses me. I often quote an adage that states, *God can hit mighty licks with crooked sticks!*

- **God is In Charge**

The Lord is in his holy temple;
    let all the earth be silent before him. Habakkuk 2:20 NIV

Despite God's silence and unusual ways, He was still in charge and in His place of authority. Therefore, keep your mouth shut and your eyes open.

LORD, I WILL PRAISE YOU

Habakkuk began in the valley by wrestling with God. He rose to be the watchtower waiting on God's reply. In the closing chapter he was on the higher ground of lofty heights. The prophet's final chapter is a poetic praise of God.

A prayer of Habakkuk the prophet. On shigionoth.
2 Lord, I have heard of your fame;
    I stand in awe of your deeds, Lord.
Repeat them in our day,
    in our time make them known;

in wrath remember mercy. Habakkuk 3:1-2 NIV

Recalling what he knew of God and His ways inspired Habakkuk to offer this *shigionoth* (poem). Indeed, what Habakkuk heard of God's fame and saw of God's awesome works now exceeded what he did not understand. His declaration echoes the lyrics of Mark Altrogge's praise song: *I stand, I stand in awe of you.* From this perspective Habakkuk offered multiple reasons to give praise to the Lord.

Praise the Lord for His Splendor

His splendor was like the sunrise;
rays flashed from his hand,
where his power was hidden. Habakkuk 3:4 NIV

A few days ago I stood on a shadowy cemetery hillside awaiting the sunrise on Resurrection Sunday. Before the sun rose, its power was hidden. In due time, it peaked over the distant horizon in full glory! Just because you do not see the sun, does not mean it has lost its splendor. It was merely hidden. Likewise, God's splendor and power may be temporarily hidden.

Praise the Lord for His Longevity

He stood, and shook the earth;
he looked, and made the nations tremble.
The ancient mountains crumbled
and the age-old hills collapsed—
but he marches on forever. Habakkuk 3:6 NIV

It is within the scope of God's power to make nations and mountains crumble. Few things appear as permanent as nations and mountains. But God can bring them to an end. On the other hand, the Lord *marches on forever.*

Consider this: Today there are millions of Jewish people still in the world. I know many of them personally. But I do not know of any Babylonians. Their empire fell away within a century of Habakkuk's prophecy. God has a much longer and grander perspective on history than humans do.

Praise the Lord for His Victory

You came out to deliver your people,
 to save your anointed one.
You crushed the leader of the land of wickedness,
 you stripped him from head to foot. Habakkuk 3:13 NIV

As God stated, He used even the wicked for His purposes. But they eventually were *crushed* and *stripped.*

Praise the Lord Anyway

In Habakkuk's closing and best-known verses, the prophet affirmed his praise to the Lord through any and every condition.

Yet I will wait patiently for the day of calamity
 to come on the nation invading us.
17 Though the fig tree does not bud
 and there are no grapes on the vines,
though the olive crop fails
 and the fields produce no food,
though there are no sheep in the pen
 and no cattle in the stalls,

> *18 yet I will rejoice in the Lord,*
> *I will be joyful in God my Savior.* Habakkuk 3:16-18 NIV

If Habakkuk only relied on his feelings and his senses, he would never have made such a great confession of faith. No matter what occurred, he said he will rejoice. In an agricultural society the loss of crops and livestock is devastating. Even so, Habakkuk could rejoice because he knew God was at work.

One of my favorite worship songs is Sinach's *Waymaker*. The "bridge" in the song declares truths that resonate with Habakkuk's message:

> *Even when I don't see it, you're workin'.*
> *Even when I don't feel it, you're workin'.*

One of the marks of great faith is a willingness to wait patiently for the Lord to work. Remember, patience is part of the Fruit of the Holy Spirit in our lives (Galatians 5:22-23).

CONCLUSION

Here are some lessons we can take and apply from Habakkuk:

- Face your doubts and ask God honest questions.
- Wait upon His reply.
- Remember God's actions.
- Focus on His assurances.
- Worship Him no matter how you feel or what you see.

Habakkuk's last words show him pressing on to God's higher ground:

The Sovereign Lord is my strength;
he makes my feet like the feet of a deer,
he enables me to tread on the heights. Habakkuk 3:19 NIV

The Lord may not immediately change the circumstances around us, but He can quickly change us to meet the circumstances. We can have faith even in the uncertainties surrounding us.

- *The opposite of faith is not doubt, but certainty. Certainty is missing the point entirely. Faith includes noticing the mess, the emptiness and discomfort, and letting it be there until some light returns.* Anne Lamott, Plan B: Further Thoughts on Faith

A Long Walk with the Minor Prophets

HOW LONG by Jeff Mowery
Sung to the tune of *How Long Has This Been Going On* written by Paul Carrack and recorded by Ace.

How long shall I keep crying on?
How long shall I keep crying on?

Well, these men with their strife and contentions
Won't admit that their breaking Your Law
Filled with violence, and trouble, and tensions
I am banging my head on the wall.

Then You said that I would be astounded.
For You'd do a work in my day.
That these Chaldean men would be coming
And destroy everything in their way!!!

How long til war is coming on?
How long til war is coming on?

Though the fig tree won't blossom like before,
And the vines won't produce any grapes,
There will be no cattle in the stalls
There'll be none that are left to escape.

Yet, I will rejoice in my great Lord!!
For He has become my Savior!!
I will choose to walk in His pure Word
The Lord God is my strength and treasure!!

And how long will sin keep going on?
How long will sin keep going on? How long?
How long will sin keep going on? How long?
How long will sin keep going on? How long?
How long will sin keep going on?

A Long Walk with the Minor Prophets

18 - HAGGAI
Haggai 1-2
More Than a Building

It's just a building. That is the kind of expression we hear when tragedy destroys a home, a school, a business, or even a church facility. Certainly, a structure pales in value when compared to a human life. Still, these places ARE more than buildings. They are spaces full of memories and feelings. They represent more than their contents.

Haggai addressed rebuilding the most important structure among the ancient Hebrews: the temple. The temple was more than a building. It represented their relationship with God.

INTRODUCTION

Moving up about 70 years from the days of Habakkuk, Haggai is the first "post exilic" prophet we have met in these studies. Thousands of Hebrews spent 50 to 70 years in exile in Babylon. During that time, prophets like Daniel and Ezekiel spoke to them.

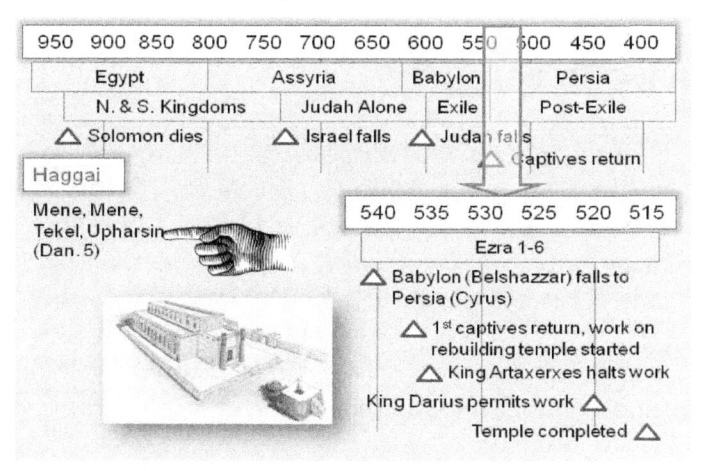

950	900	850	800	750	700	650	600	550	500	450	400
Egypt				Assyria			Babylon		Persia		
N. & S. Kingdoms				Judah Alone			Exile		Post-Exile		
△ Solomon dies				△ Israel falls		△ Judah falls					
							△ Captives return				

Haggai

Mene, Mene, Tekel, Upharsin (Dan. 5)

540	535	530	525	520	515

Ezra 1-6

△ Babylon (Belshazzar) falls to Persia (Cyrus)
△ 1st captives return, work on rebuilding temple started
△ King Artaxerxes halts work
King Darius permits work △
Temple completed △

A Long Walk with the Minor Prophets

Haggai and Zechariah probably were among the nearly 50,000 Jewish exiles who left Babylon in 537 after King Cyrus of Persia granted them permission. These repatriated Hebrews dreamed of rebuilding the temple after the Babylonians destroyed it in 587 BC. Once they arrived back in Judah, they started the project. Ezra described the launch:

But many of the older priests and Levites and family heads, who had seen the former temple, wept aloud when they saw the foundation of this temple being laid Ezra 3:12 NIV

From looking solely at the size of this foundation, these older servants knew this new temple would not compare to the size, scope, and glory of the previous temple built by Solomon 400+ years before. Unfortunately, it did not take long for their enthusiasm to cool and God's people became apathetic toward this building project. Thus, the temple construction lay unfinished until 520 BC when Haggai addressed the challenge.

The prophecies of Haggai are recorded as numerous sermons. But for our study, we will look collectively at the principles found as we read through his writing.

GIVE GOD PRIORITY

2 This is what the Lord Almighty says: "These people say, 'The time has not yet come to rebuild the Lord's house.'" 3 Then the word of the Lord came through the prophet Haggai: 4 "Is it a time for you yourselves to be living in your paneled houses, while this house remains a ruin?" Haggai 1:2-4 NIV

Today, construction delays can be caused by weather, supply chain issues, funding, or any number of variables.

What had caused the delay in the construction of the temple? God offers two basic reasons.

Excuses – *It is not time yet.*

An excuse can be defined as: *A reason wrapped around a lie.* In this situation, the lie was saying the time was not right. This was simply an empty excuse. During this period, other buildings were erected. Why not the temple? Benjamin Franklin gave this observation:

> *I never knew a man who was good at making excuses who was good at anything else.*

When you don't want to do anything, any excuse will do. Too often we make excuses when we ought to be making confession to God and practicing obedience to the Lord.

Evasion – *We busy doing something else.*

I'm too busy, is often a word I often hear when Christians are challenged to participate in Kingdom work. In Haggai's case, he revealed what activity was keeping them so busy:

"Is it a time for you yourselves to be living in your paneled houses, while this house remains a ruin?" Haggai 1:4 NIV

While there was not time to build the house of God, there WAS time to build their own houses. In fact, their homes were nicer than God's house. The Hebrews took care of their individual needs while neglecting divine requests. Their priorities were on themselves rather than the Lord. Jesus taught His followers to follow an opposite pattern.

> *Seek ye first the kingdom of God and His righteousness and all these things will be added unto you.* Matthew 6:33 KJV

The nation's priorities were confused. Often ours are too. God's work is worthy of our highest priorities.

CHANGE YOUR THINKING

In the following paragraphs Haggai challenged his people to "give careful thought" to a couple of realities and draw sound conclusions.

Think: You Are Not Getting Ahead

> *5 Now this is what the Lord Almighty says: "Give careful thought to your ways. 6 You have planted much, but harvested little. You eat, but never have enough. You drink, but never have your fill. You put on clothes, but are not warm. You earn wages, only to put them in a purse with holes in it."* Haggai 1:5-6 NIV

As hard as they worked, neglecting God's House and His ways kept them from fruitful gains and satisfaction. Jesus taught, *Where your treasure is, there your heart will be* (Matthew 6:21). Clearly, their treasure was NOT in God's work.

I believe in the biblical principle of the tithe. In this, I hold that when we tithe, God enables the remaining 90% to go further than if we kept the entire 100% to ourselves. A similar dynamic takes place here. Neglecting God's house caused the production and effectiveness of their work to decline.

It is noteworthy that Haggai did NOT advocate a "prosperity" message. Instead, He emphasized a "priority" message.

Think: You Need to Get Going

The hardest step in a formidable task is usually the first one. God told them to *get started* on the temple and understand how things work in His economy.

7 This is what the Lord Almighty says: "<u>Give careful thought</u> to your ways. 8 Go up into the mountains and bring down timber and <u>build my house</u>, so that I may take pleasure in it and be honored," says the Lord. 9 "You expected much, but see, it turned out to be little. What you brought home, I blew away. Why?" declares the Lord Almighty. "Because of my house, which remains a ruin, while each of you is busy with your own house. 10 Therefore, because of you the heavens have withheld their dew and the earth its crops. 11 I called for a drought on the fields and the mountains, on the grain, the new wine, the olive oil and everything else the ground produces, on people and livestock, and on all the labor of your hands."
Haggai 1:7-11 NIV

Here is the source of their trouble. The people were working for themselves and had no time for the Lord. Therefore, God withheld their agricultural productivity.

Several years ago I shared a unique "children's sermon" on stewardship. Holding up a beautiful red apple, I asked the boys and girls if anyone wanted this apple. A young girl quickly volunteered. But before I handed it over, I ate about half the apple in front of her. Announcing I was through with the apple, I then offered it to her. Not surprising, she no longer wanted my apple. In closing, I affirmed the point of the lesson: Christians often keep our best for ourselves and give God the leftovers. However, God is worthy of our "first fruits."

Haggai's audience needed to see that the Lord was not pleased when people neglected His house and His work while providing for themselves just fine. The way we care for God's things reflects both our spiritual priorities and the measure of our love for Him.

RESPECT THE LORD

12 Then Zerubbabel son of Shealtiel, Joshua son of Jozadak, the high priest, and the whole remnant of the people obeyed the voice of the Lord their God and the message of the prophet Haggai, because the Lord their God had sent him. And the people feared the Lord. Haggai 1:12 NIV

Haggai recognized how the people now *feared the Lord*. This expression meant they *respected the Lord* (At Last!). On twelve occasions Haggai referred to God as *the Lord Almighty* (Haggai 1:2, 5, 7, 9, 14, 2:4, 6, 7, 8, 9, 11, 23). This title reflected the rightful authority of God.

While our observation of the Sabbath provides a healthy need for renewal, any biblical interpretation encouraging God's people to be lazy instead of busy in ministry is a false interpretation and should be abandoned. Such idleness is disrespectful of the Lord.

DO NOT TRY THIS ALONE

> *Then Haggai, the Lord's messenger, gave this message of the Lord to the people: "I am with you," declares the Lord.* Haggai 1:13 NIV

As a general rule, doing difficult things is easier when someone is doing them with you. Who better to have with you than the Lord Himself? As Paul noted: *If God be for us, who can be against us?* (Romans 8:31 NIV)

DON'T BE DISCOURAGED

> *'Who of you is left who saw this house in its former glory? How does it look to you now? Does it not seem to you like nothing?* Haggai 2:3 NIV

As the book of Ezra noted, the older men seeing the foundation of this new temple looked back in discouragement. The problem with pessimism is that it is extremely contagious. This danger was part of the reasoning behind Paul's counsel to the church at Philippi: *Do everything without grumbling or arguing* (Philippians 2:14 NIV).

The restored building would not compare to the splendor of Solomon's temple, but it was still God's building. In response, Haggai offered promises from God designed to encourage the hearts of the builders.

- ***I am with you***

    Haggai repeated this promise of God he earlier stated in Haggai 1:13: *I am with you!*

    4 But now be strong, Zerubbabel,' declares the Lord. 'Be strong, Joshua son of Jozadak, the high priest. Be strong, all

A Long Walk with the Minor Prophets

you people of the land,' declares the Lord, 'and work. For I am with you,' declares the Lord Almighty. Haggai 2:4-5 NIV

Haggai emphasized the strength that accompanied the Lord's presence. To the king, to the priest, and to all the people the Lord declares the same message: *BE STRONG!* His power is the essential source of strength needed to bring about success. As the Psalmist said:

Except the LORD build the house, they labor in vain that build it: Psalm 127:1a KJV

- ### *My Glory is Coming*

  6 "This is what the Lord Almighty says: 'In a little while I will once more shake the heavens and the earth, the sea and the dry land. 7 I will shake all nations, and what is desired by all nations will come, and I will fill this house with glory,' says the Lord Almighty. Haggai 2:6-7 NIV

Contrary to common belief, bigger is not always better! You do not have to re-build what was previously built for something to be pleasing and useful to the Lord.

In my hometown, the sanctuary of a historic church burned down in the mid-1970's. Rather than rebuilding a facility that was more in keeping with their size and needs at that time and for their future, the church decided to rebuild the sanctuary exactly as it was before. Twenty years ago, my dad was interim pastor in that congregation for three years. He said he and my mom were the "youth department" of those in attendance. Members of "the old guard" were still around. They were still "idolizing" their beautiful building while decreasing in numbers. In recent years, the remaining few members gifted the building to a new and growing congregation. Thus, God's sovereign grace enabled kingdom ministry to continue in that setting. Still, I wonder how the trajectory of this congregation may have altered had they rebuilt differently.

Even to a temple seemingly inferior to its predecessor, God said, *I will fill this house with glory.* Yes! The presence of God's glory is what truly matters.

- **I Have the Materials**

'The silver is mine and the gold is mine,' declares the Lord Almighty. Haggai 2:8 NIV

Do you need precious, expensive metals to have glory? Not really. Even so, their availability is no problem to the God who owns them all.

The earth is the LORD's, and everything in it, the world, and all who live in it; Psalm 24:1 NIV

This is a good principle on stewardship: God already owns it all! It is His to supply as we need. As Paul affirmed: *And my God will meet all your needs according to the riches of his glory in Christ Jesus.* Philippians 4:19 NIV

- **Things Will Get Better**

'The glory of this present house will be greater than the glory of the former house,' says the Lord Almighty. 'And in this place I will grant peace,' declares the Lord Almighty." Haggai 2:9 NIV

Because it replaced Solomon's original "First Temple," the Hebrews referred to this smaller facility as the "Second Temple." The idea of this more modest temple receiving "greater glory" than the original surely seemed impossible to Haggai's contemporaries. What they did not know was that 400 years into the future, Herod the Great would upgrade and expand this temple significantly. But even with Herod's grand expansion, the Hebrews continued to consider this much grander structure as "The Second Temple."

Haggai's emphasis on the temple being a place God will grant "peace" is ironic. While the name "Jerusalem" literally means "City of Peace," it is historically a place known for more than its share of warfare.

IT IS EASIER TO DECLINE THAN TO RISE

I play a little game every day on my computer tablet. I found that advancing my average score is a slow and tedious process requiring many weeks of play. But when I have one bad day, my score falls to a place that literally takes months from which to recover. I consider it like rock climbing. It is tough to get higher. But a major fall can happen quickly. Haggai uses another illustration.

11 "This is what the Lord Almighty says: 'Ask the priests what the law says: 12 If someone carries consecrated meat in the fold of their garment, and that fold touches some bread or stew, some wine, olive oil or other food, does it become consecrated?'"
The priests answered, "No."
13 Then Haggai said, "If a person defiled by contact with a dead body touches one of these things, does it become defiled?"

"Yes," the priests replied, "it becomes defiled." Haggai 2:11-13 NIV

Haggai makes the point that consecration (or *holiness*) does not transfer from one object to another, but defilement does. A similar comparison regards hygiene. When you shake someone's hand with your clean hand, your cleanness does not transfer to the other person. However, if your hand is dirty, your dirt DOES transfer to that person.

Haggai gave this word of application:
Then Haggai said, "'So it is with this people and this nation in my sight,' declares the Lord. 'Whatever they do and whatever they offer there is defiled. Haggai 2:14 NIV

Diligence is required to remain holy and consecrated before the Lord. Sin, on the other hand, is easily spread.

VICTORY IS AHEAD

22 I will overturn royal thrones and shatter the power of the foreign kingdoms. I will overthrow chariots and their drivers; horses and their riders will fall, each by the sword of his brother. Haggai 2:22 NIV

As with other prophets, the ultimate attention rests on the work of the Lord. Notice the use of the phrase *I will* in regard to the victory God intended to achieve.

Haggai closed, interestingly, on a favorable note regarding Zerubbabel, the king of the Hebrews:

23 "'On that day,' declares the Lord Almighty, 'I will take you, my servant Zerubbabel son of Shealtiel,' declares the Lord, 'and I will

make you like my signet ring, for I have chosen you,' declares the Lord Almighty." Haggai 2:23 NIV

In reality, Zerubbabel was a humble governor of a struggling remnant of the Jewish nation. It was a difficult situation for him. Therefore, God gave him this word of encouragement about the future. As the Lord's chosen *signet ring* Zerubbabel marked God's authority. From our side of the New Testament, we see how Zerubbabel held a space in the line of David that eventually lead to Jesus.

After the exile to Babylon:
Jeconiah was the father of Shealtiel,
Shealtiel the father of Zerubbabel,
13 Zerubbabel the father of Abihud, Matthew 1:12-13a NIV

the son of Joanan, the son of Rhesa,
the son of Zerubbabel, the son of Shealtiel, Luke 3:27a NIV

How this message must have encouraged Zerubbabel and his people to stay on the job and finish the work God gave them to do!

CONCLUSSION - LESSONS TO LEARN

Keep your priorities in order.

Preference for themselves caused negligence to their service to the Lord.

Work together.

Work with one another and work with God. I like an adage I heard years ago regarding cooperating Christian ministries: *We ain't fighting nobody but the devil.*

Indeed, as Paul recorded: *For we are laborers <u>together</u> with God.* 1 Corinthians 3:9a KJV

Trust in the Lord.

His strength, His supply, and His help will bring His success.

Don't stop until you finish.

They started rebuilding the temple but stopped for the better part of 16 years. Haggai admonished them to restart and to press onward. Work with devotion. Sin is transferable and can pull you down quickly. Ezra recorded the completion of the temple construction:

So the elders of the Jews continued to build and prosper under the preaching of Haggai the prophet and Zechariah, a descendant of Iddo. They finished building the temple according to the command of the God of Israel and the decrees of Cyrus, Darius and Artaxerxes, kings of Persia. Ezra 6:14 NIV

As we recognized at the first: The temple was much more than just a building to their ancient faith.

Two years ago, my congregation was approaching our 85th Anniversary. It was a noteworthy date I knew we should not let pass without some recognition. I have a pastor friend in Raleigh, North Carolina named Jeff Roberts. Dr. Robert's niece, Emily Ann Roberts, had achieved quite a bit of notoriety as a contestant on the television show *The Voice*. One day Jeff posted a video of Emily Ann, singing at The Grand Ole Opry. The song was one she composed about her home church building. Watching that video made me cry because I recognized people in my church could resonate with the lyrics. My first thought was to have someone in my church sing this song. Then God gave me a bigger idea. Because I personally knew someone with direct connections to Emily Ann Roberts, I could ask her to sing at my church! A couple of emails later I was talking on the telephone with her booking agent. Everything fell into place. She gave a great concert with us on our anniversary Sunday. The climax was when she sang *The Building* written about her home church. Here is the chorus.

I know the stained glass never saved a soul
And these pews ain't on the roll that's called up yonder
I know the pulpit's just a wooden stand
But it's felt the power of God's hand
As His glory filled the place with awe and wonder
I know it's just a buildin', plain and simple white
But it's the buildin' where Jesus changed my life.
-Emily Ann Roberts

YOUR HOUSE by Jeff Mowery
Sung to the tune of *Our House* written by Graham Nash and recorded by Crosby, Stills, and Nash.

I sent My fire
When they built the Temple
In Jerusalem that day.
Off'rings on the fire, for hours and hours
While I listened to them sound their praises
All day long for Me, only for Me.

Come to Me now, and finish what you
Started back then
Everything's not done.
My Temple's a ruin, with no illumination
By My Spirit's presence 'cause you have built
Lovely homes for you, only for you.

Your house, is a very, very, very, fine house.
With panels on the walls,
From cedars that were tall.
And everything was easy 'cause of Me
You sang "la, la, la, la, la……."

My House should be a sacred, holy House
With altars and incense
A desire for My presence
With sacrifice and praise that comes from you

And then…

I'll send My fire when you build a house worthy for Me this very day.

19 – Zechariah
Chapters 1-6
Trust the Lord

This week I heard an interview with retired Pittsburg Steelers football coach Bill Cowher. Coach Cowher discussed his approach for motivating athletes: *Some players need to be encouraged and some players need to be yelled at.* While many of the prophets seem to "yell" direct messages from the Lord, Zechariah takes a more *encouraging* approach. The repatriated Hebrews were a small, weak remnant of people facing the monumental task of rebuilding a nation with few available resources. They needed vision and inspiration for the challenge before them.

INTRODUCTION

Several characteristics of Zechariah are worthy of note:

- Meaning "The Lord Remembers," the name "Zechariah" is the most common name in the Hebrew Bible. My research found between 27 and 33 different people in the Bible named Zechariah.

- Like Haggai, Zechariah likely was born during the Babylonian captivity and travelled with Zerubbabel and the other Jews who were permitted to resettle to Judah in 536 B.C.

- Zechariah was a priest. The book's opening verse identifies the priestly line of his family:

In the eighth month of the second year of Darius, the word of the Lord came to the prophet Zechariah son of Berekiah, the son of Iddo: Zechariah 1:1 NIV

A Long Walk with the Minor Prophets

The key is Zechariah's father, Iddo. He is listed in Nehemiah 12:4 as a priest who returned from exile with king Zerubbabel. That same chapter recognizes Zechariah as a head of a priestly family (Nehemiah 12:16). Thus, Zechariah was from a priest AND carried the duties of a prophet. This is a rare combination. Samuel, Ezekiel, and John the Baptist are among the few in the Bible identified with both these functions.

- The reference *to the second year of Darius* dates Zechariah's prophecy about 520 BC.

- With 14 chapters, Zechariah matches Hosea as the longest of the minor prophets. His words are quoted or alluded to at least 40 times in the New Testament.

There are three major divisions in this book. We will cover each one over the next three lessons. This study outlines the first six chapters under three headings. Each affirms the trustworthiness of the Lord.

REPENTANCE

Repentance is a major part of restoration with the Lord. When Jesus inaugurated His public ministry, He declared:

"The time has come," he said. "The kingdom of God has come near. Repent and believe the good news!" Mark 1:15 NIV

Repentance is often associated with emotional regret. But this spiritual endeavor also involved action.

Repentance Comes with Change

> *Therefore tell the people: This is what the Lord Almighty says: 'Return to me,' declares the Lord Almighty, 'and I will return to you,' says the Lord Almighty.* Zechariah 1:3 NIV

In our last study, Haggai told his contemporaries to "look around" at what was not working for them. God was withholding fruitfulness because they neglected the spiritual devotion necessary to rebuild the temple. Zechariah, on the other hand, told the Hebrews to "look back" at what went wrong with the generations before them.

> *4 Do not be like your ancestors, to whom the earlier prophets proclaimed: This is what the Lord Almighty says: 'Turn from your evil ways and your evil practices.' But they would not listen or pay attention to me, declares the Lord. 5 Where are your ancestors now? And the prophets, do they live forever? 6 But did not my words and my decrees, which I commanded my servants the prophets, overtake your ancestors?* Zechariah 1:4-6 NIV

The phrase *I told you so* is often delivered with an attitude of superiority and smugness. But here, the tone communicates sadness over the poor choices of earlier generations. Prophet after prophet called them out for their idolatry, injustice, and trust in things other than the Lord. But they did not pay attention to the Lord's words and were *overtaken* by them. Now it was up to Zechariah's audience to respond with change.

Repentance Comes with Promises

There are two promises here worth affirming.

-You have the opportunity – *Where are your ancestors now?* Zechariah 1:5a NIV

> They are dead. They were victims of their failure to repent. Zechariah's generation had the opportunity to experience a far better fate.

-You have the presence/power of the Lord – *I will return to you.* Zechariah 1:3b NIV

> In His judgment, God previously allowed His people to follow their own waywardness. This was why they experienced so much trouble. Genuine repentance would bring assurance of God's active engagement with His people.

Repentance Requires a Response

> *"Then they repented and said, 'The Lord Almighty has done to us what our ways and practices deserve, just as he determined to do.'"* Zechariah 1:6b NIV

> *Confession* is defined as simply *agreeing with God*. This confessional statement shows these Hebrews agreed with God about their sin and God's discipline. In my childhood, I did not get disciplined for everything I did wrong. But I earnestly believe I deserved every punishment I did receive. The Hebrews humbly recognized their guilt. True repentance honestly acknowledges we are ALWAYS in need of repentance and grace.

There is a story about a group of Christians discussing what they believed God will say to them when they arrive in heaven. On participant offered, *I think God will say to me, "Why didn't you let me bless you like I wanted to?"* Our failure to repent reduces the availability of God's gracious handiwork in our lives.

ENCOURAGEMENT

In the heart of this first section, Zechariah detailed a series of eight visions. These revelations encouraged the Hebrews by representing favorable ways God's "return to them" would take place.

1. Horsemen

8 During the night I had a vision, and there before me was a man mounted on a red horse. He was standing among the myrtle trees in a ravine. Behind him were red, brown and white horses. Zechariah 1:8 NIV

10 Then the man standing among the myrtle trees explained, "They are the ones the Lord has sent to go throughout the earth." 11 And they reported to the angel of the Lord who was standing among the myrtle trees, "We have gone throughout the earth and found the whole world at rest and in peace." Zechariah 1:10-11 NIV

For many generations the Hebrews lived under the shadow of warfare. The horsemen's "report" of peace coming to earth was very welcome news.

12 Then the angel of the Lord said, "Lord Almighty, how long will you withhold mercy from Jerusalem and from the towns of Judah, which you have been angry with these seventy years?" 13 So the Lord spoke kind and comforting words to the angel who talked with me. Zechariah 1:12-13 NIV

How long? is a regular question addressed to God. Remember Habakkuk asked *How long* his prayers would go unanswered and *How long* injustice would continue (Habakkuk 1:1).

Zechariah's vision reported an encouraging reply to the angel's inquiry:

16 "Therefore this is what the Lord says: 'I will return to Jerusalem with mercy, and there my house will be rebuilt. And the measuring line will be stretched out over Jerusalem,' declares the Lord Almighty.
17 "Proclaim further: This is what the Lord Almighty says: 'My towns will again overflow with prosperity, and the Lord will again comfort Zion and choose Jerusalem.'" Zechariah 1:16-17 NIV

Notice God's response does NOT answer the original question of *How long?* Still, this was a beautiful promise of what was ahead. When our situations are discouraging, remember how God identifies with our sufferings and oversees the future.

2. Horns and Craftsmen

18 Then I looked up, and there before me were four horns. 19 I asked the angel who was speaking to me, "What are these?" He answered, "These are the horns that scattered Judah so that no one could raise their head, but the craftsmen have come to terrify them and throw down these horns of the nations who lifted up their horns against the land of Judah to scatter its people." Zechariah 1:18-19a, 20b NIV

Persecution has scattered the Hebrew people throughout much of their history. As a result, they often lived as a small minority with difficult circumstances. In this vision, the kingdoms scattering Judah are represented by four horns. I suspect these horns represent the four domains in Daniel's prophecy typically translated as the Babylonia, Persian, Greek, and Roman empires. Each ascended to power and was "thrown down" by the "craftsmen" who engineered the succeeding empire. Yet throughout the rise and fall of so many kingdoms, God protected the Hebrew people from annihilation. Herein lies their hope. If God did not have a plan for their future, He could have allowed them to disappear from history.

3. Measuring Line

Then I looked up, and there before me was a man with a measuring line in his hand. 2 I asked, "Where are you going?" He answered me, "To measure Jerusalem, to find out how wide and how long it is." Zechariah 2:1-2 NIV

Do you know the square footage of your home? You probably do. But do you know the square footage of anyone else's home? Probably not. The reason we know the square footage of our home is simple: It is OUR home. Zechariah saw God measuring Jerusalem. The vision said to the Hebrews, *Your city is God's home.*

- **The city is going to be bigger than its walls.**

Jerusalem will be a city without walls because of the great number of people and animals in it. 5 And I myself will be a wall of fire around it,' declares the Lord, 'and I will be its glory within.' Zechariah 2:4b-5 NIV

In Zechariah's time, Jerusalem's population was small and weak. But God promised a day when the city's walls could not contain all its citizenry. Today, modern Jerusalem extends far beyond the ancient walls to the old city. Primary centers of government and commerce operate outside the ancient walls of Old Jerusalem.

- **Others should join in.**

7 "Come, Zion! Escape, you who live in Daughter Babylon!" 8 For this is what the Lord Almighty says: "After the Glorious One has sent me against the nations that have plundered you—for whoever touches you touches the apple of his eye— 9 I will surely raise my hand against them so that their slaves will plunder them. Then you will know that the Lord Almighty has sent me. Zechariah 2:7-9 NIV

Many Hebrews who lived in Babylon did not return from exile with Haggai and Zechariah. They had settled into Babylon and lacked confidence in the future of Jerusalem. Zechariah encouraged them to return. A secure future was with those called *the apple of God's eye*. There was no future in Babylon. The Lord would cause those who plundered Jerusalem (Babylon) to themselves be plundered!

The Lord will inherit Judah as his portion in the holy land and will again choose Jerusalem. Zechariah 2:12 NIV

I include this verse because it holds a unique characterization: While we use the phrase "The Holy Land" regularly to identify Israel, this is the only place in the Bible where Palestine is referred to as "The Holy Land."

4. The High Priest Cleansed

Then he showed me Joshua the high priest standing before the angel of the Lord, and Satan standing at his right side to accuse him. 2 The Lord said to Satan, "The Lord rebuke you, Satan! The Lord, who has chosen Jerusalem, rebuke you! Is not this man a burning stick snatched from the fire?" Zechariah 3:1-2 NIV

The fourth vision pictured a courtroom scene. Joshua, the high priest, represents the Hebrew people. *Satan* stands in an *adversarial role* accusing Joshua of wrongs. When the Lord's verdict is announced, Satan is the one rebuked. Jerusalem, like a stick snatched from the flames of a fire, is liberated. The weight of the verdict in Jerusalem's favor falls not because of the people's worthiness. Instead, they are saved simply because the Lord *has chosen Jerusalem.*

3 Now Joshua was dressed in filthy clothes as he stood before the angel. 4 The angel said to those who were standing before him, "Take off his filthy clothes." Then he said to Joshua, "See, I have taken away your sin, and I will put fine garments on you." Zechariah 3:3-4 NIV

God is in the clothing business. He clothed Adam and Eve in garments made of skins (Genesis 3:21). Isaiah states, *For he has clothed me with garments of salvation and arrayed me in a robe of his righteousness* (Isaiah 61:10 NIV). An old hymn declares the holy garments awaiting us as His people:

> *Dressed in His righteousness alone, faultless to stand before the throne.*
> —Edward Mote, 1834

This is another encouraging word! God forgives and cleanses His people.

5. The Gold Lampstand and Olive Trees

Then the angel who talked with me returned and woke me up, like someone awakened from sleep. 2 He asked me, "What do you see?" I answered, "I see a solid gold lampstand with a bowl at the top and seven lamps on it, with seven channels to the lamps. 3 Also there are two olive trees by it, one on the right of the bowl and the other on its left." Zechariah 4:1-3 NIV

Within the Holy Place in the tabernacle stood a golden candlestick with seven branches (Exodus 25:31-40). It was the high priest's duty each morning and evening to trim the wicks and provide the oil needed to keep the lamp burning (Leviticus 24:2-4). In the 2nd century BC, the seven-branched candlestick became more familiar through the origin of Hanukkah. Today, it is a symbol of the modern state of Israel.

The vision of the lampstand assured Zechariah's generation of the future rebuilding and restoration of the temple. Still, the primary resource for this construction was not found within this world.

6 So he said to me, "This is the word of the Lord to Zerubbabel: 'Not by might nor by power, but by my Spirit,' says the Lord Almighty. Zechariah 4:6 NIV

Solomon built his temple by the power of a strong economy. The Babylonians destroyed the temple by the power of their military. These Hebrews had neither an army nor prosperity. Nevertheless, the Spirit of the Lord Almighty was enough.

12 Again I asked him, "What are these two olive branches beside the two gold pipes that pour out golden oil?" 13 He replied, "Do you not know what these are?" "No, my lord," I said. 14 So he said, "These are the two who are anointed to serve the Lord of all the earth." Zechariah 4:12-14 NIV

The two Olive Trees *anointed to serve the Lord* affirmed Joshua the High Priest and Zerubbabel the King. These two played key roles in the restoration of Judah.

6. The Flying Scroll

I looked again, and there before me was a flying scroll. 2 He asked me, "What do you see?" I answered, "I see a flying scroll, twenty cubits long and ten cubits wide."

3 And he said to me, "This is the curse that is going out over the whole land; for according to what it says on one side, every thief will be banished, and according to what it says on the other, everyone who swears falsely will be banished. Zechariah 5:1-3 NIV

The sheer size of this scroll was impressive. Twenty cubits by ten cubits translates to thirty-five feet by seventeen feet. Still, its messages were short and simple: a curse against those who steal on one side and a curse against those who swear falsely on the other. Thus, the scroll covered the eighth and ninth Commandments: *Thou shall not steal* and *Thou shall not bear false witness.* By contrast, modern culture affirms "commands" such as: *Thou shalt not get caught!* This vision encouraged the Hebrews by affirming the forthcoming arrival of God's justice.

7. A Lady in a Basket

> *5 Then the angel who was speaking to me came forward and said to me, "Look up and see what is appearing." 6 I asked, "What is it?" He replied, "It is a basket." And he added, "This is the iniquity of the people throughout the land."*
> *7 Then the cover of lead was raised, and there in the basket sat a woman! 8 He said, "This is wickedness," and he pushed her back into the basket and pushed its lead cover down on it.* Zechariah 5:5-8 NIV

In this vision, wickedness is represented by a woman. During the class discussion of verse six several ideas were suggested for the reason a woman would represent wickedness. Some thought she may represent Eve's role in original sin. Another person reminded us the church is "the bride of Christ" and therefore feminine. Several of my resources proposed that wickedness is represented by a woman because the Hebrew word for *wickedness* is feminine.

The verses that follow give a fitting response: The wickedness represented by a woman was removed by women.

> *Then I looked up—and there before me were two women, with the wind in their wings! They had wings like those of a stork, and they lifted up the basket between heaven and earth. 10 "Where are they taking the basket?" I asked the angel who was speaking to me. 11 He replied, "To the country of Babylonia to build a house for it. When the house is ready, the basket will be set there in its place."* Zechariah 5:9-11 NIV

The reference to female angels is rare in scripture. But it is these *women with wings* who carry wickedness to its fitting home in Babylon.

8. The Four Chariots

I looked up again, and there before me were four chariots coming out from between two mountains—mountains of bronze. 2 The first chariot had red horses, the second black, 3 the third white, and the fourth dappled—all of them powerful. 4 I asked the angel who was speaking to me, "What are these, my lord?"

5 The angel answered me, "These are the four spirits of heaven, going out from standing in the presence of the Lord of the whole world. 6 The one with the black horses is going toward the north country, the one with the white horses toward the west, and the one with the dappled horses toward the south." Zechariah 6:1-6 NIV

Zechariah's final vision returned to the image of horses. In chapter one, horses went out to report the condition of the earth. Here, these chariots work to accomplish God's purposes. Traditionally, these colors represent certain disasters (see Revelation 6:1-8)

Red = Warfare
Black = Famine
White = Death
Dappled (Spotted) = Plague

The cumulative message of this vision declared God's judgment upon the Gentile nations for their sins. Consequences of misdeeds headed out in every direction.

COMMISSION

God had assured the Hebrews He would cleanse them, protect them, deliver them, and judge their enemies.

Chapter six closes with one further assurance: The Messiah would arrive.

11 Take the silver and gold and make a crown, and set it on the head of the high priest, Joshua son of Jozadak. 12 Tell him this is what the Lord Almighty says: 'Here is the man whose name is the Branch, and he will branch out from his place and build the temple of the Lord. Zechariah 6:11-12 NIV

In the introduction to this study, we recognized how, on rare occasions, a person could be both priest and prophet. Zechariah himself held both these roles. But here a priest was also crowned as king! This was not possible. In ancient Israel, a priest could not be king. Priests came from the tribe of Levi while kings originated from the line of Judah.

The reference points to an even higher priest who would come. This coronation belonged to the coming Messiah who was to be a temple Himself. This temple would be destroyed and rebuilt in three days (Matthew 26:61, Mark 14:58, John 2:19). Jeff Mowery, one of my church members, affirmed this interpretation noting the Hebrew equivalent for the name "Jesus" is "Joshua." Both mean *The Lord is Salvation.*

13 It is he who will build the temple of the Lord, and he will be clothed with majesty and will sit and rule on his throne. And he will be a priest on his throne. And there will be harmony between the two.' Zechariah 6:12-13 NIV

The Bible's three great Messianic titles are *Prophet, Priest, and King*. God's people should be encouraged! A Savior is coming who uniquely and distinctively embraces all three roles.

A Long Walk with the Minor Prophets

Crown Him! Crown Him! Prophet, and Priest, and King! – Fanny Crosby, 1869

20 – Zechariah
Chapters 7-8
Traditions and Promises

One of the signature songs from the musical *Fiddler on the Roof* affirms the traditions practiced by a Jewish community residing in Imperial Russia during the early 1900's. The drama traces the struggle of questioning and even abandoning several long-standing traditions.

Congregations are full of "traditions." Here is a partial list of traditions observed by the church where I serve along with an approximate date they began.
Annual Thanksgiving Dinner (way back!)
Easter Sunrise Service (way back!)
Christmas Eve Service (early 1970's)
Hanging of the Green Service (Early 1990's)
Campfire Worship Night (Mid 1990's)
Patriotic Service (2004)
Good Friday Service (2010)

In addition, churches follow other "unofficial" traditions like the typical order of service, the location people tend to sit in the sanctuary, the time-of-day when church gatherings take place, and many more. The presence of religious traditions creates a number of questions.

HOW LONG DOES IT TAKE FOR SOMETHING TO BECOME A TRADITION?

The simple answer is, *At least once.*

Tim Paul is a church orchestration minister who grew up in the church I pastor. During his college years at the University of Tennessee he was part of their *Pride of the Southland Marching Band*. During his tenure, the band added a pause on their gameday march to the football stadium. They played a set of several fight songs called *The Salute to the Hill.* After the first occurrence the campus police told the band they could not do that because it severely backed up traffic. The band responded by saying *The Salute to the Hill* must go on because *It is a Tradition!* So I guess something can become a tradition even after its inaugural occurrence.

The tradition addressed in Zechariah 7 originated some 70 years before. Thus, they were deeply rooted.

HOW LONG SHOULD A TRADITION CONTINUE?

The word *Tradition* means *that which is passed along.* At what point does a tradition no longer need to be passed along. When should a tradition end? THIS is the question addressed to Zechariah.

In the fourth year of King Darius, the word of the Lord came to Zechariah on the fourth day of the ninth month, the month of Kislev. 2 The people of Bethel had sent Sharezer and Regem-Melek, together with their men, to entreat the Lord 3 by asking the priests of the house of the Lord Almighty and the prophets, "Should I mourn and fast in the fifth month, as I have done for so many years?" Zechariah 7:1-3 NIV

A bit of background helps us understand the inquiry.

First, the designation *the fourth year of King Darius* tells us two years have passed since Zechariah's opening chapter. During the Hebrew's time in exile, four new fasts were added to the religious calendar. These fasts commemorated tragic events surrounding the destruction of Jerusalem and the temple. In particular, the fifth month fast commemorated the burning of the temple. Now the messengers present this question: *Since the temple was being rebuilt, do we need to keep up the fast traditionally observed during the fifth month.*

In response, Zechariah does something very *Hebrew-ish*: He answers a question with a series of questions.

Who Is This For?

4 Then the word of the Lord Almighty came to me: 5 "Ask all the people of the land and the priests, 'When you fasted and mourned in the fifth and seventh months for the past seventy years, was it really for me that you fasted? 6 And when you were eating and drinking, were you not just feasting for yourselves? Zechariah 7:4-6 NIV

If the practice of a tradition is essential for your worship experience, ask yourself who the tradition is meant to benefit. The primary object of worship focuses on God alone. Yet, we occasionally hear statements like:

- *I cannot worship ....if we don't sing the doxology...* or *...at this new time of service...* or *unless the preaching is fiery.*

But worship is not about the one doing the worshipping. Worship is for the Lord. The response question states: *Are these traditions for you or for Him?* Every Sunday morning I post the same statement on my Facebook page: **Come Let Us Worship the Lord!** We are not called together to be entertained or even to get our needs met. We gather to offer worship and praise to the Lord. *Traditionalism* is going through the outward motions instead of honoring the Lord from our heart.

Time and again we read in the Bible where God desires more than "going through the traditional motions" such as offering temple sacrifices:

> *"Does the Lord delight in burnt offerings and sacrifices*
> *as much as in obeying the Lord?* 1 Samuel 15:22 NIV

> *"I have more than enough of burnt offerings,*
> *of rams and the fat of fattened animals;*
> *I have no pleasure*
> *in the blood of bulls and lambs and goats.* Isaiah 1:11b NIV

> *Shall I come before him with burnt offerings,*
> *with calves a year old?*
> *He has shown you, O mortal, what is good.*
> *And what does the Lord require of you?*
> *To act justly and to love mercy*
> *and to walk humbly with your God.* Micah 6:6,8 NIV

God had made his priorities clear. Frankly, it is much easier to maintain traditions than to really meet God, share a heart experience with Him, and carry out ministry that makes an impact. The Lord must be the center of our lives and the reason for our actions.

The ultimate answer to the messenger's inquiry to Zechariah is found in the next chapter. All four fasts will one day turn into festivals as times of grief transform into occasions for rejoicing.

19 This is what the Lord Almighty says: "The fasts of the fourth, fifth, seventh and tenth months will become joyful and glad occasions and happy festivals for Judah. Therefore love truth and peace." Zechariah 8:19 NIV

What Honors the Lord?

8 And the word of the Lord came again to Zechariah: 9 "This is what the Lord Almighty said: 'Administer true justice; show mercy and compassion to one another. 10 Do not oppress the widow or the fatherless, the foreigner or the poor. Do not plot evil against each other.' Zechariah 7:8-10 NIV

God called His people to practice justice and compassion. The words of the prophets condemn exploitation for personal gain and the failure to show compassion to widows, orphans, and aliens.

What Angers the Lord?

11 "But they refused to pay attention; stubbornly they turned their backs and covered their ears. 12 They made their hearts as hard as flint and would not listen to the law or to the words that the Lord Almighty had sent by his Spirit through the earlier prophets. So the Lord Almighty was very angry. Zechariah 7:11-12 NIV

They responded they refused to listen. Rather than change, they covered their ears and made their hearts like flint. They chose cold traditions that failed to bring about transforming change. Dead traditions easily can become roadblocks to progress.

What Are the Consequences?

13 "'When I called, they did not listen; so when they called, I would not listen,' says the Lord Almighty. 14 'I scattered them with a whirlwind among all the nations, where they were strangers. Zechariah 7:13-14 NIV

God says, *Since you do not listen to me, I will not listen to you.* I know folks who hardly ever answer a call to their cell phone. When these same folks call me, I often lack motivation to answer them. Agree with me or disagree with me. But do not ignore me!

What a frightening thought of God turning His back and refusing to answer us. Yet, God's discipline may simply allow the natural consequences of our sins to fall upon us. Three times in Romans 1:24-28 it states, *God gave them over....*

PROMISES

In chapter eight Zechariah transitioned to words of promise for the Hebrews to remember. Traditions look to the past. Promises turn attention to the future. These promises would bring genuine hope and enlighten devotion to the Hebrews far beyond their outward practices of tradition.

The Promise of Restoration

The key to restoration was not reconstruction. Rather, it was the presence of the Lord.

3 This is what the Lord says: "I will return to Zion and dwell in Jerusalem. Then Jerusalem will be called the Faithful City, and the mountain of the Lord Almighty will be called the Holy Mountain." Zechariah 8:3 NIV

A popular television show in the 1970's was *The Six Million Dollar Man*. During the opening, a description of the "rebuilding" of astronaut Steve Austin included the line *We can make him better than he was before Better...Stronger...Faster.*

God's promise was not just to restore Jerusalem, but to rebuild it better with faithful people and as a holy mountain. The imagery went on to describe a city of peace and tranquility.

4 This is what the Lord Almighty says: "Once again men and women of ripe old age will sit in the streets of Jerusalem, each of them with cane in hand because of their age. 5 The city streets will be filled with boys and girls playing there." Zechariah 8:4-5 NIV

The promised city would be so safe and friendly the elderly could leisurely sit in the streets and talk, and the children could play in the streets and not be in danger.

The Promise of Regathering

7 This is what the Lord Almighty says: "I will save my people from the countries of the east and the west. 8 I will bring them back to live in Jerusalem;" Zechariah 8:7-8a NIV

A taste of this experience has occurred following the establishment of the nation of Israel in 1948. Jewish people from all over the world with education, resources, skills, and passion continue to immigrate into Israel.

Around 15 years ago I led a group on a tour of Israel. On previous visits to Israel our tour guides were people with long residencies in Palestine. But on this tour our guide was a native of western New York state who had relocated to Israel. She was one, like the prophet described, who felt called to return to live in Jerusalem.

The Promise of Relationship

For a time, God had abandoned (ignored) His people because they had ignored Him. But this was only temporary.

they will be my people, and I will be faithful and righteous to them as their God. Zechariah 8:8b NIV

Remember Hosea renamed his child *Lo-Ammi* (*Not My* Child) into *My People* (Hosea 2:23). Similarly, Zechariah reports God reclaiming these people as His own.

The Promise of Refreshment

Zechariah presents a before/after contrast. Here is the "Before:"

Before that time there were no wages for people or hire for animals. Zechariah 8:10a NIV

Haggai's prophecy noted how God prevented the ground from producing fruitfulness because the people neglected the work on the temple. Despite their efforts, the economy could never get going.

In contrast, now God says the ground WILL be fruitful to the remnant.

12 "The seed will grow well, the vine will yield its fruit, the ground will produce its crops, and the heavens will drop their dew. I will give all these things as an inheritance to the remnant of this people. Zechariah 8:12 NIV

A quick reminder: Do not obey God just to become wealthy. We never have that kind of leverage on the Lord. Also, God does not always respond to our faithfulness with monetary blessings. He may instead grant health, friendships, relationships, community, influence, peace of mind, or any other means of kindness in response to our devotion.

The Promise of Renewed Standards

God admonished His people regarding their obligations to speak the truth, to practice justice in the courts, to honor His name, and to love their neighbors.

These are the things you are to do: Speak the truth to each other, and render true and sound judgment in your courts; 17 do not plot evil against each other, and do not love to swear falsely. I hate all this," declares the Lord. Zechariah 8:16-17 NIV

In the past, they failed to practice these standards. Now they were to "up their game" by eliminating the things God hated. It may honestly feel as if ethics and standards only slide downward. But it is possible for true believers to improve the moral temperature of society. When the modern missionary movement took the gospel to the world, they built schools, hospitals, and raised the moral practices of the land. This was the workings of the Lord.

The Promise of the Nation's Redemption

Israel had failed to be a blessing to the nations God designed it to be. But Zechariah promised the desire of nations would be to entreat the Lord.

20 This is what the Lord Almighty says: "Many peoples and the inhabitants of many cities will yet come, 21 and the inhabitants of one city will go to another and say, 'Let us go at once to entreat the Lord and seek the Lord Almighty. I myself am going.' 22 And many peoples and powerful nations will come to Jerusalem to seek the Lord Almighty and to entreat him." Zechariah 8:20-22 NIV

We routinely put a message before our congregation that simply says: *The church exists for those who do not attend it.* Believers need this reminder because we can make ministry all about us. God's desire is to go to the nations:

2 In the last days
the mountain of the Lord's temple will be established
    as the highest of the mountains;
it will be exalted above the hills,
    and <u>all nations will stream to it</u>. Isaiah 2:2 NIV

On each side of the river stood the tree of life, bearing twelve crops of fruit, yielding its fruit every month. And the leaves of the tree are for the <u>healing of the nations</u>. Revelation 22;2 NIV

THE GOSPEL IS ATTRACTIVE

23 This is what the Lord Almighty says: "In those days ten people from all languages and nations will take firm hold of one Jew by the hem of his robe and say, 'Let us go with you, because we have heard that God is with you.'" Zechariah 8:23 NIV

What an amazing promise! God's blessings will be so great, others eagerly will desire the kind of relationship with the Heavenly Father they witness in His people. One of my church's members is a dear lady named Janelle Martin. Janelle volunteers with a wonderful ministry to women who are incarcerated. Recently she talked about a prisoner who attended a spiritual weekend provided by this ministry. The inmate stated her motivation to attend with these words: *I want what you ladies have.*

For I am not ashamed of the gospel, because it is the power of God that brings salvation to everyone who believes: first to the Jew, then to the Gentile (Romans 1:16 NIV). May the Lord allow our lives to be a powerful tool God uses to reach people all around us.

21 – Zechariah
Zechariah 9-14
The King Has Come, and the King is Coming

During my youth, my home church put on a grand Christmas worship experience. It featured a Living Christmas Tree occupied with scores of young singers. The worship minister behind it all was Bruce Forlines. Bruce's signature solo was his own version of Bill and Gloria Gather's *The King Is Coming*. My Dad was pastor and asked Bruce to sing *The King is Coming* as the closing song of the The Living Christmas Tree. When Bruce inquired how a Christmas worship time could include a song about the return of the Lord, Dad replied *I will take care of that*. Thus, near the end, after my father's challenge to those in attendance to trust Jesus, he transitioned into Bruce's song with these simple words: *The King has come, and the King is Coming*.

Zechariah's closing chapters cover both the first and second coming of Jesus. In essence, he declares *The King is coming and The King is coming again!* The prophet alternates between the humility of Jesus' incarnation and the grandeur of His future return. For our purposes, we will assemble individually Zechariah's references to the first and the second appearances of the Messiah.

THE FIRST COMING

While the Hebrews commonly believed their forthcoming Messiah would be a grand, royal, and/or military leader, God's actual plans included the arrival of someone much lowlier in nature.

The Humble Servant

Rejoice greatly, Daughter Zion!

Shout, Daughter Jerusalem!
See, your king comes to you,
righteous and victorious,
lowly and riding on a donkey,
on a colt, the foal of a donkey. Zechariah 9:9 NIV

It is easy to recognize the fulfillment of this prophecy from Jesus' entry into Jerusalem on Palm Sunday. An invading king's arrival on an impressive steed would bring fear and intimidation. But King Jesus' unpretentious arrival called for rejoicing.

The Rejected Savior/Shepherd

7 So I shepherded the flock marked for slaughter, particularly the oppressed of the flock. Then I took two staffs and called one Favor and the other Union, and I shepherded the flock. The flock detested me, and I grew weary of them and said, "I will not be your shepherd. Zechariah 11:7, 8b NIV

Even though the Messiah would come for those "oppressed," Zechariah prophesied He would not be accepted. During His earthly ministry, Jesus noted His destiny was *to suffer much and be rejected* (Mark 9:12b). Isaiah portrayed this same dismissal:

He was despised and rejected by mankind, a man of suffering, and familiar with pain. Like one from whom people hide their faces he was despised, and we held him in low esteem. Isaiah 53:3 NIV

Zechariah continued, noting the consequences of their rejection.

> *10 Then I took my staff called Favor and broke it, revoking the covenant I had made with all the nations. 11 It was revoked on that day....* Zechariah 11:10-11a NIV

Following the crucifixion of Jesus, Jew and Gentile came to faith in the same way: through faith in Jesus. Remember, at the death of Jesus, the veil of the temple was torn in two. This miracle signified that a restored relationship with God no longer required the activity of the temple. In a sense, the *favored* status of the Hebrew religion was removed.

> *12 I told them, "If you think it best, give me my pay; but if not, keep it." So they paid me thirty pieces of silver. 13 And the Lord said to me, "Throw it to the potter"—the handsome price at which they valued me! So I took the thirty pieces of silver and threw them to the potter at the house of the Lord.* Zechariah 11:12-13 NIV

The ultimate rejection is betrayal. This prophecy was fulfilled when Judas betrayed Jesus for 30 pieces of silver. This money ultimately bought a potter's field (Matthew 27:1-10).

THE SECOND COMING

Much within Zechariah's closing chapters refer to the great and final return of the Lord. The phrase "on that day" appears 18 times in Zechariah with 16 of them coming in the final three chapters.

Earlier Zechariah received a variety of visions to encourage the Hebrews (Zechariah 1-6). Here he shares numerous images of the great and coming King.

The Peacemaker

I will take away the chariots from Ephraim
and the warhorses from Jerusalem,
and the battle bow will be broken.
He will proclaim peace to the nations.
His rule will extend from sea to sea
and from the River to the ends of the earth. Zechariah 9:10 NIV

In His return, Jesus will be the ultimate Prince of Peace. Militaries will be disarmed as peace extends throughout the nations. Zechariah's prophecy echoes the sentiments of Isaiah:

He will judge between the nations
and will settle disputes for many peoples.
They will beat their swords into plowshares
and their spears into pruning hooks.
Nation will not take up sword against nation,
nor will they train for war anymore. Isaiah 2:4 NIV

The Storm

Then the Lord will appear over them;
his arrow will flash like lightning.
The Sovereign Lord will sound the trumpet;
he will march in the storms of the south,
and the Lord Almighty will shield them. Zechariah 9:14-15a NIV

Thunderstorms arrive with foreboding power and imposing fanfare. They are loud and unpredictable. The final appearance of the Lord will share these characteristics. The book of Revelation refers to the sound of a trumpet 15 times. While we usually associate storms with their destructive power, this storm shields God's people against their enemies.

The Supplier

*They will destroy
and overcome with slingstones.* Zechariah 9:15b

Victory is supplied! Translations differ on whether this victory is won using slingstones or against an enemy using slingstones. Ultimately, this does not matter. God's powerful presence enables His people to experience victory. Therefore, as the adage says, *To the victor goes the spoils:*

*They will drink and roar as with wine;
they will be full like a bowl
used for sprinkling the corners of the altar.* Zechariah 9:15b NIV

Many folks may have enjoyed a meal at the Pennsylvania Amish country restaurant named *The Good and Plenty*. I have taken a few groups there myself. I always encourage people to try to arrive hungry! As the name declares, there was going to be an abundance of great food. *Good and Plenty* is also a description of the Messiah's supply. Paul affirmed the same to the Philippians:

And my God will meet all your needs according to the riches of his glory in Christ Jesus. Philippians 4:19 NIV

The Shepherd

The Lord their God will save his people on that day as a shepherd saves his flock. Zechariah 9:16a NIV

The Lord as a shepherd is a familiar image.

- Jesus called Himself the Good Shepherd who *lays down His life for the sheep* (John 10:11).
- The beloved psalm declared *The Lord is my Shepherd* (Psalms 23:1).
- Jesus' familiar parable described God as a devoted shepherd determined to rescue even a single sheep lost among a flock of 100 sheep (Luke 15:3-7).

During these studies we have seen many prophecies against poor leaders. Zechariah includes this judgment against people in power who failed at their *shepherding* duties:

"Woe to the worthless shepherd,
who deserts the flock! Zechariah 11:17a NIV

The word *worthless* indicates *corrupt* leaders who, unlike the good shepherd, do not care for the people they oversee. Instead, their only concern is for themselves.

The Jeweler

They will sparkle in his land
like jewels in a crown.
17 How attractive and beautiful they will be! Zechariah 9:16b-17a NIV

Because precious stones are rare and unique, they possess great value. But their "rough" appearance may not be impressive. Therefore, a keen eye is required to recognize gems and their worth. The

Hebrews were often rebellious and irreverent to the Lord. Yet, His ultimate assessment saw them as treasured stones fit to be crown jewels.

The Leader/Transformer

"My anger burns against the shepherds,
and I will punish the leaders;
for the Lord Almighty will care
for his flock, the people of Judah,
and make them like a proud horse in battle. Zechariah 10:3 NIV

If Jesus is the good shepherd, His followers are His flock. Isaiah stated the same: *We all like sheep have gone astray* (Isaiah 53:6a). Frankly, sheep do not project an image of power, courage, or strength. However, our Messiah will transform meek sheep into proud warhorses. That is quite a transformation.

The Restorer

I admire people who restore things like old cars, houses, artwork, and furniture. The returning Messiah will perform an even more difficult task. He will restore PEOPLE.

I will restore them
because I have compassion on them.
They will be as though
I had not rejected them,
for I am the Lord their God
and I will answer them. Zechariah 10:6b NIV

Part of this restoration is returning (restoring) His people to their land. While persecution may have dispersed the Hebrews throughout the world, the return of the Messiah will lead them home in mass.

They and their children will survive,
*   and they will return.*
10 I will bring them back from Egypt
*   and gather them from Assyria.*
I will bring them to Gilead and Lebanon,
*   and there will not be room enough for them.* Zechariah 10:9b-10 NIV

The Deliverer

While the Lord restores people, He delivers Jerusalem. In fact, Jerusalem is mentioned more than 20 times in the final three chapters of Zechariah.

2 "I am going to make Jerusalem a cup that sends all the surrounding peoples reeling. Judah will be besieged as well as Jerusalem. 3 On that day, when all the nations of the earth are gathered against her, I will make Jerusalem an immovable rock for all the nations. All who try to move it will injure themselves. Zechariah 12:2-3 NIV

There is a long history of hostility in Palestine. Therefore, it is not hard to imagine the spark of history's mighty and final war taking place around Jerusalem. Yet the Lord will stand at the city's defense.

4 On that day I will strike every horse with panic and its rider with madness," declares the Lord. "I will keep a watchful eye over Judah, but I will blind all the horses of the nations. 5 Then the clans of Judah will say in their hearts, 'The people of Jerusalem are strong, because the Lord Almighty is their God.' Zechariah 12:4-5 NIV

3 Then the Lord will go out and fight against those nations, as he fights on a day of battle. Zechariah 14:3 NIV

Notice the phrase, *I will*. Deliverance is God's work. In his familiar battle against Goliath, David confidently declared his arsenal included the power of the Lord.

David said to the Philistine, "You come against me with sword and spear and javelin, but I come against you in the name of the Lord Almighty, the God of the armies of Israel, whom you have defied. 1 Samuel 17:45 NIV

My sister Jan plays doubles tennis in a lady's league. I recently told her my secret to success in doubles tennis: play with a really good partner. It was once said that the greatest doubles tennis team in the world was whoever was playing with John McEnroe! Likewise, it is a great thing to be on the side of the Lord.

The Cleanser

10 "And I will pour out on the house of David and the inhabitants of Jerusalem a spirit of grace and supplication. They will look on me, the one they have pierced, and they will mourn for him as one mourns for an only child, and grieve bitterly for him as one grieves for a firstborn son. Zechariah 12:10 NIV

It starts with an acknowledgement of sin. Notice the spirit of repentance. These people now recognize the one who was *pierced* and grieve His loss. Thus, *grace and supplication* (forgiveness) are poured out. John's first epistle gave this assurance:

If we confess our sins, he is faithful and just and will forgive us our sins and purify us from all unrighteousness. 1 John 1:9 NIV

In 1772 William Cowper penned his hymn beginning with these lyrics.

> *There is a Fountain filled with blood drawn from Immanuel's veins.*
> *And sinners plunged beneath that flood lose all their guilty stains.*

It is said he based this hymn upon this verse:

On that day a fountain will be opened to the house of David and the inhabitants of Jerusalem, to cleanse them from sin and impurity. Zechariah 13:3 NIV

The Refiner

> *I will refine them like silver*
>   *and test them like gold.*
> *They will call on my name*
>   *and I will answer them;*
> *I will say, 'They are my people,*
>   *and they will say, 'The Lord is our God.'"* Zechariah 13:9 NIV

Refinement is part of the purification process. The impurities burn off leaving the untainted metal behind. Before, Zechariah grieved the people's failure to communicate with God (Zechariah 7:13). Now, refinement will restore communication along with the intimate affirmations of *my people* and *our God* (Zechariah 8:8).

The Healer

6 On that day there will be neither sunlight nor cold, frosty darkness. 7 It will be a unique day—a day known only to the Lord—with no distinction between day and night. When evening comes, there will be light.
8 On that day living water will flow out from Jerusalem, half of it east to the Dead Sea and half of it west to the Mediterranean Sea, in summer and in winter. Zechariah 14:6-8 NIV

The scene mirrors the picture in Revelation 22 of the new Jerusalem. In that eternal city there is no darkness (Revelation 22:5) and a river of life runs through the center (Revelation 22:2).

The One and Only King

The Lord will be king over the whole earth. On that day there will be one Lord, and his name the only name. Zechariah 14:9 NIV

Zechariah foretells the same circumstances declared in the familiar words of Paul:

that at the name of Jesus every knee should bow,
 in heaven and on earth and under the earth,
11 and every tongue acknowledge that Jesus Christ is Lord,
 to the glory of God the Father. Philippians 2:10-11 NIV

Zechariah closes his portrayal of *on that day* emphasizing the complete and ultimate holiness of the Lord:

20 On that day holy to the Lord will be inscribed on the bells of the horses, and the cooking pots in the Lord's house will be like the sacred

A Long Walk with the Minor Prophets

bowls in front of the altar. 21 Every pot in Jerusalem and Judah will be holy to the Lord Almighty, and all who come to sacrifice will take some of the pots and cook in them. Zechariah 14:20-21a NIV

Zechariah began with a call to repentance but ended with a vision of glory. Every item will be considered *holy* and *sacred* because everything will be transformed and made holy when the victorious King returns.

Indeed, from our perspective, *The King Has Come* and *The King Is Coming*.

ZECHARIAH by Jay McCluskey
Sung to the tune of *Y.M.C.A.* written by Jacques Morali and Victor Willis, and recorded by The Village People.

Young man, born in ole Babylon
I said, young man, now it's time to move on
I said young man, head to your folk's hometown
There's a word you have to give them.

Young man, Tell them all to repent.
I said, young man, all their chances aren't spent
They can change ways, and turn all things about.
There is hope for life with no doubt.

They need a word from God, Zechariah
They need a word from God, Zechariah

You are prophet and priest
from the great to the least
They'll be coming back from west and the east

They need a word from God, Zechariah
They need a word from God, Zechariah

I can help them get clean.
I can give them new clothes.
And vict'ry over all of their foes.

Visions, of horses and olive trees
And more visions, even stranger than these.
All to give hope that their God's in control.
He is Prophet, Priest, and Great King.

Answers, of traditions and ways
They say, Help us, should they go or just stay?
Are they for Me, or just for their own cause.

A Long Walk with the Minor Prophets

When I call they put me on pause!

They need a word from God, Zechariah
They need a word from God, Zechariah

You are prophet and priest
from the great to the least
They'll be coming back from west and the east

They need a word from God, Zechariah
They need a word from God, Zechariah

I can help them get clean.
I can give them new clothes.
And vict'ry over all of their foes.

Tell them, of a forthcoming king
Mighty Power, Grace, and Peace He will bring
First a shepherd, humble and rejected.
But on that day He's exalted!

That's when, all that's broke is restored.
I say, That's when, I'm no longer ignored.
They'll be one Lord and only one name
Every tongue confess and proclaim!

They need a word from God, Zechariah
They need a word from God, Zechariah

You are prophet and priest
from the great to the least
They'll be coming back from west and the east

Zechariah
They need a word from God, Zechariah

A Long Walk with the Minor Prophets

Young man, young man,
There's no need to feel down.
Young man, young man, we're on Holy Ground

Zechariah
They need a word from God, Zechariah

Young man, young man, help them listen to me.
Young man, young man. They'll see great victory!
Zechariah

A Long Walk with the Minor Prophets

22 – Malachi
Malachi 1-2
Get Back in Your Lane

In Aledous Huxley's novel, Brave New World, the character named Fanny Crowne declares: *Ending is better than mending.*

We have arrived at the book of Malachi, the *ending* point of the twelve Minor Prophets. Yet, after 400 years of prophecy, there remains much *mending* to be done between the Hebrews and the Lord.

INTRODUCTION

The name Malachi means "My Messenger." It is a fitting name for the final prophet of our study. In a sense, every prophet was the Lord's *messenger*. Malachi also spoke of another *messenger* who would come and prepare the way for the Lord. Finally, Malachi reiterates many of the same warnings and dangers addressed by his fellow prophets.

We prefer to be a "messengers" good news. But this is not always the word the Lord needs delivered. For God's people…

> *Sometimes our message is to comfort the afflicted.*
> *Other times our message is to afflict the comfortable.*

Malachi, and many of the other prophets, fell into this second category. His words pointed out the failings of the Hebrew people in his day.

Malachi spoke to the exiles some 100 years after their initial return to Judah. It was beyond the days of Zechariah and Haggai. Malachi's ministry took place either at the time of Nehemiah or shortly afterwards. Unlike some other prophets, we know nothing about his life, his family, or his vocation.

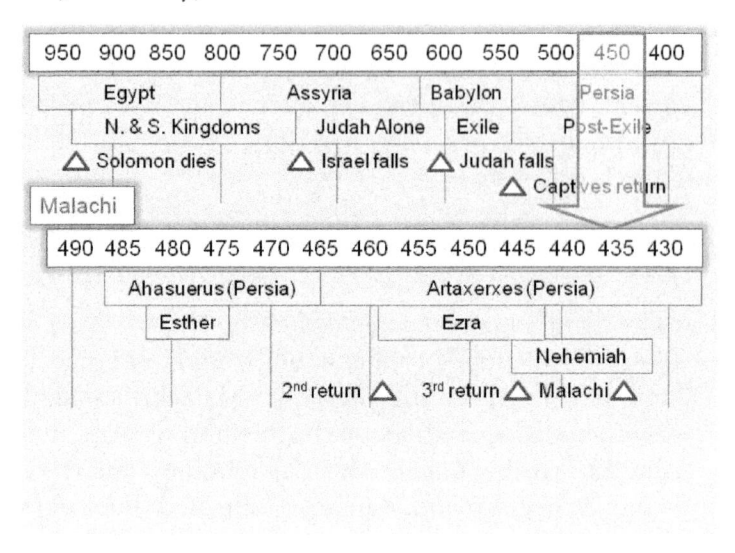

950	900	850	800	750	700	650	600	550	500	450	400
	Egypt				Assyria		Babylon			Persia	
	N. & S. Kingdoms				Judah Alone		Exile			Post-Exile	
	△ Solomon dies				△ Israel falls		△ Judah falls				
								△ Captives return			
Malachi											

490	485	480	475	470	465	460	455	450	445	440	435	430
	Ahasuerus (Persia)						Artaxerxes (Persia)					
	Esther						Ezra					
									Nehemiah			
			2nd return △			3rd return △	Malachi △					

The return of the exiled people to Jerusalem brought some significant and positive reforms. But eventually things began to decline and fall apart. The Hebrews fell into some of the same mistakes of their ancestors. They were about to drift *out of their lane* of devotion to the Lord.

By now, the temple was rebuilt, the sacrificial system was reestablished, and the festivals were resumed. Still, the dramatic promises of prophets like Haggai and Zechariah were far from fulfilled. The nation was discouraged and disappointed by what they felt were unfulfilled promises. This led them to a lower regard and disrespect for God. Israel needed an assurance of God's love and a challenge to obey. Malachi directed them to *Get Back in Your Lane* by honoring and obeying the Lord.

A prophecy: The word of the LORD to Israel through Malachi. Malachi 1:1 NIV

The word *prophecy* here is translated often as *oracle* or *burden*. This term communicates the heaviness of these messages. Overall, Malachi's prophecy is divided into six *oracles*. We will cover three in this lesson and three in our closing session.

As we look at each one, notice how Malachi's words tend to follow a pattern:
- He makes a statement from God.
- A question is replied.
- An answer to the question is given.

Oracle 1: DENYING GOD'S LOVE FOR YOU

Life was hard. The blessings, productivity, prosperity, and fruitfulness promised by other prophets had not materialized. Thus, the Hebrews declined into a conviction that God did not care about them. God responds with a clear statement of His love:

2 "I have loved you," says the Lord.
"But you ask, 'How have you loved us?'
"Was not Esau Jacob's brother?" declares the Lord. "Yet I have loved Jacob, 3 but Esau I have hated, and I have turned his hill country into a wasteland and left his inheritance to the desert jackals." Malachi 1:2-3 NIV

Here you see the statement – question – answer format in this oracle.

The Hebrews were not confident God loved them. They replied with the question, *How?* Malachi pointed out God's love through His *choice* of their ancestor Jacob.

God chose Jacob instead of his brother Esau to carry the blessing promised to their grandfather Abraham. In some ways, Esau appeared to be the more likely candidate. Though Jacob and Esau were twins, Esau was born first. Nevertheless, Jacob was chosen even before he and Esau were born:

> *"Two nations are in your womb,*
> *and two peoples from within you will be separated;*
> *one people will be stronger than the other,*
> *and the older will serve the younger."* Genesis 25:23 NIV

God did not hate Esau in the sense of cursing him or striking out against him. Indeed, Esau was a blessed man (Genesis 33:9, 36:1-43). Yet when God chose Jacob, this left Esau *unchosen*.

Do not think of "hate" as a statement of God's wrath and animosity. It is better understood that Esau was "less loved." God's love for Jacob was so great that, in comparison, His actions toward Esau looked like hatred. Jesus incorporated similar language when He stated His followers must "hate" their own family:

> *If anyone comes to me and does not hate father and mother, wife and children, brothers and sisters—yes, even their own life—such a person cannot be my disciple.* Luke 14:26 NIV

Oracle 2: SINS OF THE PRIESTS

This "heavy message" deals with stewardship. The Mosaic Law clearly prohibited offering blemished sacrifices to the Lord.

> *Do not bring anything with a defect because it will not be accepted on your behalf.* Leviticus 22:20 NIV

> *If an animal has a defect, is lame or blind or has a serious flaw, you must not sacrifice it to your lord.* Deuteronomy 15:21 NIV

In Malachi's day, the priests, who were supposed to honor God's name, were disgracing it by offering defiled sacrifices to Him.

> *"It is you priests who show contempt for my name.*
> *"But you ask, 'How have we shown contempt for your name?'*
> *7 "By offering defiled food on my altar.*
> *"But you ask, 'How have we defiled you?'*
> *"By saying that the Lord's table is contemptible. 8 When you offer blind animals for sacrifice, is that not wrong? When you sacrifice lame or diseased animals, is that not wrong? Try offering them to your governor! Would he be pleased with you? Would he accept you?" says the Lord Almighty.* Malachi 1:6-8 NIV

Here we get the DOUBLE oracle formula: Statement-Question-Answer-Question-Answer. The Hebrews inquire about the source of their contempt followed by a question asking how they defiled the Lord.

No ministry rises any higher than its leaders. Quality leadership sets the bar that others follow. By permitting this contemptuous practice, rather than inspiring the people to a higher way, the priests caused people to stumble.

> *7 "For the lips of a priest ought to preserve knowledge, because he is the messenger of the Lord Almighty and people seek instruction from his mouth. 8 But you have turned from the way and by your teaching have caused many to stumble;* Malachi 2:7-8 NIV

No genuine follower wants to be a stumbling block to another person. Paul instructed the church at Rome regarding this danger:

> *Instead, make up your mind not to put any stumbling block or obstacle in the way of a brother or sister.* Romans 14:13b NIV

But in Malachi's day, allowing worshippers to bring less than their best created a stumbling block rather than a stimulation.

Years ago, I heard Paul Harvey tell a story about the Butterball Turkey hotline receiving a call. The inquirer asked if it would be safe to cook and eat a turkey that has been in their freezer for 15 years. The support-line person said technically it would be safe. But, that long in a freezer would cause the turkey to lose most of its flavor. The caller replied, *That is what we thought too. We'll give it to the church.*

Beware when we design, prefer, or insist upon worship/ministry practices that cost us little to nothing. Jesus taught this way to assessing our values:

> *For where your treasure is, there your heart will be also.* Matthew 6:21 NIV

When we keep our treasures for ourselves, we show our priorities.

If such a defective gift would not be acceptable to the Governor, what made the people think it was pleasing to the Lord? Instead, such an offering reduced their standing with the Lord to the realm of chicanery.

> *Cursed is the cheat who has an acceptable male in his flock and vows to give it, but then sacrifices a blemished animal to the Lord.* Malachi 1:14 NIV

The word *cheat* is the Hebrew word "nakal" which translates as *deceiver* or *swindler*.

Looking ahead to the end times, God declares the full and proper expression of His greatness:

> *My name will be great among the nations, from where the sun rises to where it sets. In every place incense and pure offerings will be brought to me, because my name will be great among the nations," says the Lord Almighty.* Malachi 1:11 NIV

This is a glorious promise that the true worship of God one day will extend over all the earth.

Oracle 3: UNFAITHFULNESS TO THE COVENANT

> *11 Judah has been unfaithful. A detestable thing has been committed in Israel and in Jerusalem: Judah has desecrated the sanctuary the Lord loves by marrying women who worship a foreign god. 12 As for the man who does this, whoever he may be, may the Lord remove him from the tents of Jacob—even though he brings an offering to the Lord Almighty.* Malachi 2:11-12 NIV

This wording format lacks a question after the initial statement in v. 11. But inquiries are implied: *How have we been unfaithful?* Or *What detestable thing have we done?* The answer: Men were divorcing their wives to marry pagan women. This practice negatively affected so many dynamics of their discipleship and home.

Becoming *Unequally Yoked* with Foreign Wives

The scriptures taught the error of this practice for multiple generations.

- Israel married women from Moab and brought the curse of God upon the people (Numbers 25).

- Solomon married foreign women who took his heart away from God (1 Kings 11:1-10).

- Ahab married Jezebel – a foreign woman given over to pagan gods – who led Israel into new depths of depravity (1 Kings 16:29-33).

- Paul says that believers and unbelievers should not be joined together (2 Corinthians 6:11-18).

In the study of Zechariah, we referred to the musical *Fiddler on the Roof* and its theme of *tradition*. The tradition this story most emphasized was the parents' arrangement of their children's marriages. The main character, Tevye, is conflicted when his daughters instead want to marry for love. He breaks tradition and allows his oldest two daughters to marry their choice in husbands. But the third daughter crossed a line when she chose to marry a husband who did not share their faith.

Interfaith marriages can work. But there likely is more of an **acceptance** of each other's religious convictions rather than a collective effort to **advance** a common faith.

Leaving Women as Helpless Victims

"For I hate divorce!" says the LORD, the God of Israel. "To divorce your wife is to overwhelm her with cruelty," says the LORD of Heaven's Armies. "So guard your heart; do not be unfaithful to your wife." Malachi 2:16 NLT

We have all witnessed the fracture and difficulty of broken and failed marriages. In Old Testament society, essentially only men could divorce a woman. Women, on the other hand, had very few avenues to divorce a husband. If divorced by her husband, a woman often faced devastating circumstances.

Notice the phrase, *overwhelm her with cruelty*. Some English versions utilize the phrase *covers with violence*. Today, we give a wedding ring to symbolize a covenant. In ancient Israel, a groom placed a corner of his garment over her to symbolize the coverage of his protection. Divorce, on the other hand, exposed her to cruel treatment.

Damaging Their Relationship with God

These problems affected the genuineness of their worship. They went through the right motions, but there was no response from the Lord.

13 Another thing you do: You flood the Lord's altar with tears. You weep and wail because he no longer looks with favor on your offerings or accepts them with pleasure from your hands. 14 You ask, "Why?" It is because the Lord is the witness between you and the wife of your youth. You have been unfaithful to her, though she is your partner, the wife of your marriage covenant. Malachi 2:13-14 NIV

Their worship became an empty ritual that they engaged in more to maintain tradition than to please a holy and righteous God. In Matthew 6, Jesus spoke of insincere praying, giving, and fasting. Doing these actions merely to promote a false impression grants no spiritual impact.

Our relationships with people influence the health of our relationship with God. Remember, Jesus spoke of laying your gift to God down and seeking reconciliation with your brother before returning to make reconciliation with the Lord (Matthew 5:23-24).

Less Likely to Produce Godly Children

Didn't the LORD make you one with your wife? In body and spirit you are his. And what does he want? Godly children from your union. So guard your heart; remain loyal to the wife of your youth. Malachi 2:15 NLT

God had called Israel to be unique because He had a special task for them and their descendants:

6 These commandments that I give you today are to be on your hearts. 7 Impress them on your children. Talk about them when you sit at home and when you walk along the road, when you lie down and when you get up. Deuteronomy 6:6-7 NIV

Simply speaking, their marriages with pagans were less likely to produce children with a strong faith in the Lord. By contrast, believers in the God of Abraham hold that children are a blessing. They are made in the image of God for the purpose of helping the world be closer to the Lord's design.

Article 16 of the Universal Declaration of Human Rights describes the family as *the natural and fundamental unit of society*. Indeed, the family is the nucleus of a sound civilization. This complements well the teachings of scripture: The first and foremost way God organized people was by putting them into families. Many of our cultural problems will decline when the quality of homes improves. By God's own design, the world becomes a better place with solid families and marriages that honor Him.

A Long Walk with the Minor Prophets

23 – Malachi
Malachi 3-4
Easy Doesn't Change the World

In our previous study we examined the first three "heavy" oracles Malachi delivered to the Hebrews:

- Questioning God's love.
- Allowing inferior offerings to the Lord.
- Marriages outside the faith.

One hundred years following their return from exile, the Hebrew people still were struggling. The initial enthusiasm of their return from Babylon was replaced with frustrations about the hardships of their lives. A college football player commented that all the emotional fire and enthusiasm built up in the locker room before the game quickly goes away once you have received a couple of hard licks on the playing field. Afterwards, toughness is required to continue.

The Hebrew's enthusiasm was gone, and times remained tough. Consequently, the people in Malachi's day, like many of their ancestors, became slack in their devotion to the Lord. They wanted life to be easy and go more to their own liking. In my research, I found a book by John D. Barry on Malachi with a title reflecting the prophets reply to their lackadaisical attitude: *Easy Doesn't Change the World*. This study will review Malachi's final three oracles to the Hebrews.

Oracle 4 – QUESTIONING GOD'S JUSTICE

17 You have wearied the Lord with your words.
"How have we wearied him?" you ask.
By saying, "All who do evil are good in the eyes of the Lord, and he is pleased with them" or "Where is the God of justice?" Malachi 2:17 NIV

Again, we find Malachi's signature format: God makes a statement. This statement is followed by a question from the people. In replay, God responds with an explanation of their offense.

God is omnipotent with all power. Therefore, He does not grow weary. However, He says here He does grow tired of this blasphemous accusation about His injustice: *The Lord likes the wicked people!*

The Hebrews came back to Palestine, rebuilt the temple, and restored their worship. But they still experienced difficulties. Therefore, they said: *Where is the justice in that?* However, they did not need God's justice. They needed mercy and forgiveness. Malachi answered the question *Where is the God of justice?* By speaking about two messengers.

A Message of Mercy

> *"I will send my messenger, who will prepare the way before me. Then suddenly the Lord you are seeking will come to his temple; the messenger of the covenant, whom you desire, will come,"* says the Lord Almighty. Malachi 3:1 NIV

The gospels identify this first messenger as John the Baptist (Mark 1:2). John the Baptist links the close of the old covenant with the beginning of the new. He is referenced in the closing chapters of Malachi, and he is featured at the beginning of all four gospel accounts.

The "messenger of the covenant" foretells the coming of Jesus, the one they ultimately desire and need to make things right. How does this verse answer the question of where God's justice is? When Jesus came and died on the cross, He completely satisfied the justice of God. That covenant, based on mercy, was the justice they desired.

A Message of Cleansing

2 But who can endure the day of his coming? Who can stand when he appears? For he will be like a refiner's fire or a launderer's soap. 3 He will sit as a refiner and purifier of silver; he will purify the Levites and refine them like gold and silver. Malachi 3:2-3a NIV

A variety of expressions are made here regarding cleansing: *Fire, Soap, Refiner,* and *Purifer.* We have seen similar images of refinement in previous oracles and prophecies. But note who are being purified: *Levites,* the priestly tribes. Remember, Malachi's second oracle condemned the priests for offering defective sacrifices. The Levites needed cleansing! Following this purification, a different quality of offerings will occur:

Then the Lord will have men who will bring offerings in righteousness, 4 and the offerings of Judah and Jerusalem will be acceptable to the Lord, as in days gone by, as in former years. Malachi. 3:3b-4 NIV

Sacrificial offerings of lame and blind animals were not suitable to their governor, much less the Lord Almighty. But after this cleansing, *righteous* and *acceptable* offerings once again will be given.

Oracle 5 – ROBBING GOD

Return to me, and I will return to you," says the Lord Almighty.

> *"But you ask, 'How are we to return?'*
> *8 "Will a mere mortal rob God? Yet you rob me.*
> *"But you ask, 'How are we robbing you?'*
> *"In tithes and offerings. 9 You are under a curse—your whole nation—because you are robbing me. 10 Bring the whole tithe into the storehouse, that there may be food in my house. Test me in this,"* *says the Lord Almighty, "and see if I will not throw open the floodgates of heaven and pour out so much blessing that there will not be room enough to store it.* Malachi 3:7b-10 NIV

God's call for His people to *return* brought out a question of *How?* God's reply referred to their "robbing" Him. This in turn initiated a repeat of the inquiry *How?* His answer: Their crime was withholding their tithes. The giving of a tenth as an act of worship was as old as Abraham, who tithed to Melchizedek (Hebrews 7:2). Tithing was incorporated into the Law of Moses in several places, including:

A tithe of everything from the land, whether grain from the soil or fruit from the trees, belongs to the LORD; it is holy to the LORD. Leviticus 27:30 NIV

By failing to tithe, the Hebrews were not only robbing God, they also were robbing themselves. They were closing the floodgates of heaven's blessings. People who believe in and practice the Biblical standard of tithing trust that the pouring out of the Lord's blessings will far outweigh their gift.

I know of a young Christian who found himself in a financial tight spot. In search of relief, he considered discontinuing his giving to the church. A wise mentor gave him this biblical counsel: *You will not save money by stopping your tithing.* While tithing is counter-intuitive, faithful stewards believe God's promise to bless our giving actually surpasses what we give in our worship offerings. Thus, tithing is a spiritual issue more than a financial one.

Greed indicates a weak relationship with God. Jesus quoted Deuteronomy saying it was forbidden to put God to the test (Matthew 4:7, Deuteronomy 6:16). But here, God actually invites us to test Him on this and see if His blessings do not exceed our generosity.

Oracle 6 – DESPISING SERVICE TO GOD

I get tired in the work, but I never get tired of the work. –Dwight L. Moody

13 "You have spoken arrogantly against me," says the Lord. "Yet you ask, 'What have we said against you?' 14 "You have said, 'It is futile to serve God. What do we gain by carrying out his requirements and going about like mourners before the Lord Almighty? 15 But now we call the arrogant blessed. Certainly evildoers prosper, and even when they put God to the test, they get away with it.'" Malachi 3:13-14 NIV

Things that give us "pause for concern" sometimes are referred to as "red flags." These verses reveal a couple of "red flags" regarding the spiritual walk of the Hebrews. The expression *What do we gain?* reveals their *What's in it for me?* attitude. They were not interested in honoring God! Their perspective was selfish. Notice also the words describing the spirit of their worship: *going about like mourners.* God's people are commanded to *Serve the Lord with gladness* (Psalm 100:2). Instead, they preferred to have life go their own way and complain when it did not.

To disobedient Hebrews, it seemed the arrogant prospered whereas the righteous were considered poor and despised for their ignorance and foolishness. Malachi gave assurance that, while these genuine and faithful believers were in the minority, God recognized their devotion. These worshippers met together not to complain but to encourage and to edify each other. God took notice and promised to remember them:

A scroll of remembrance was written in his presence concerning those who feared the Lord and honored his name. 17 "On the day when I act," says the Lord Almighty, "they will be my treasured possession. I will spare them, just as a father has compassion and spares his son who serves him. Malachi 3:16b-17 NIV

It is great to feel treasured. Dr. Andy Lester was one of my favorite seminary professors in the field of pastoral counseling. I remember his observation that all the well-balanced people he knew had something in common: During their formative years, there was someone in their lives who adored them. Ultimately, our worth and self-esteem is grounded in this truth: God treasures us.

The prophet goes on to speak of a coming day when all things will be set right. The wicked will wane while the faithful will flourish:

All the arrogant and every evildoer will be stubble, and the day that is coming will set them on fire," says the Lord Almighty. Malachi 4:1b NIV

But for you who revere my name, the sun of righteousness will rise with healing in its rays. And you will go out and frolic like well-fed calves. Malachi 4:2 NIV

Finally, Malachi closes his prophecies with a look back and a look forward. These final verses are like an appendix to

Malachi's oracles. Notice these words do not follow the statement-question-reply format found with the six oracles.

The reader is first instructed to look back to Moses.

> *Remember the law of my servant Moses, the decrees and laws I gave him at Horeb for all Israel.* Malachi 4:4 NIV

The law of Moses was and would continue to be the guiding rule of life.

Afterwards, the writing looks forward to a coming Elijah.

> *5 "See, I will send the prophet Elijah to you before that great and dreadful day of the Lord comes. 6 He will turn the hearts of the parents to their children, and the hearts of the children to their parents; or else I will come and strike the land with total destruction."* Malachi 4:5 NIV

The featured part of the Lord's healing is the restoration of families. The home is a model of the kingdom of God. Again, the first way God organized people was through the creation of homes. Healthier homes make the world closer to God's design.

Together, Moses and Elijah represent the two great divisions of the Old Testament: The Law and The Prophets. The Law gave God's instructions while the Prophets called God's people back from their erroneous ways. It is no coincidence that these two figures appeared with Jesus on the Mount of Transfiguration. Jesus was the fulfillment of both the Law and the Prophets.

The stark expression *OR ELSE* communicates a sense of ultimatum. The result is going one way or another! Hearts either are turned *or else* there is judgment/curse.

The closing phrase of *total destruction* is translated *curse* in about half of the English translations I reviewed. It is an interesting way to close the book and the Old Testament. But the *curse* of sin remained until Jesus came and defeated it.

In the Introduction of this book, we noted that prophets were both forthtellers and foretellers.

Malachi was a *Forthteller* in the sense that he identified the wrongs of the people.
Malachi was a *Foreteller* in that he prophesized the coming of the Lord.

Therefore, the Old Testament ends in a bit of a *cliff hanger*: *Which way will it go?* The people tried to argue back to God. But the Lord always has the last word. Prayerfully, we will respond to Him in such a way that His last word to us will be one of salvation and not judgment.

A Long Walk with the Minor Prophets

DO IT GOD'S WAY by Jay McCluskey
Sung the tune of *I Did It My Way* as written by Paul Anka and recorded by Frank Sinatra.

And now, the end is near
And so you'll hear the final prophet
My friends, I'll say it clear
I'll state God's case on every topic
You've lived a life that's tough
You're now in doubt and deepest dismay
I'm Malachi, Here is God's word:
"Don't do it your way!"

Mistakes, you've made a few
But of all these, there's six I'll mention
Deny my love. Offer the lame.
No worthy gift was your intention.
God planned a better course
For every step on life's great highway
But less, much less than this
You did it your way

So many times, you failed God's lead
Sin came to tempt. You went with greed
And left your spouse for pagan wives
You robbed your God, withheld your tithes
Then wondered how, life got so foul
You did it your way!

You gave, you worked and served
At qualities of your low standards
"God is not fair." "The wicked thrive."
"To serve is waste." Among your slanders
God knows, remembers all
Who feared and honored Him all day
Those treasured souls, spared and consoled

A Long Walk with the Minor Prophets

They did it God's way!

There's coming a man, a great messenger
To declare truth and prepare another
Who will come quick, purify and reverse
Set families right and remove the curse
The record shows. He'll take our blows.
And do it God's Way!

Printed in Great Britain
by Amazon